A Leader's Guide to Cybersecurity

A Leader's Guide to Cybersecurity

WHY BOARDS NEED TO LEAD—
AND HOW TO DO IT

Thomas J. Parenty | Jack J. Domet

Harvard Business Review Press
Boston, MA

The web addresses referenced in this book were live and correct at the time of the book's publication but may be subject to change.

Library of Congress Cataloging-in-Publication Data

Names: Parenty, Thomas J., author. | Domet, Jack J., author.
Title: A leader's guide to cybersecurity : why boards need to lead–and how to do it / Thomas J. Parenty, Jack J. Domet.
Description: Boston, MA : Harvard Business Review Press, [2019]
    | Includes index. |
Identifiers: LCCN 2019025243 | ISBN 9781633697997 (hardback) |
    ISBN 9781633698000 (ebook)
Subjects: LCSH: Computer security. | Boards of directors. | Organizational behavior. | Business planning.
Classification: LCC QA76.9.A25 P375 2019 | DDC 005.8–dc23
LC record available at https://lccn.loc.gov/2019025243

The paper used in this publication meets the requirements of the American National Standard for Permanence of Paper for Publications and Documents in Libraries and Archives Z39.48-1992.

To Copernicus

Contents

Part Three
The Responsibilities

Part Four
The Aides

A Leader's Guide to Cybersecurity

Introduction

Digital Stewardship

Over the past decade, as the world has become more digital, companies, governments, and organizations have spent billions of dollars on cybersecurity. Yet, as their investments have grown, the financial consequences of cyber breaches have increased, seemingly in lockstep.

Open a newspaper, anywhere in the world, and you'll probably find a story of a cyberattack that had devastating consequences. Recent examples include a 2016 cyber heist at Bangladesh Bank (the central bank of Bangladesh) that resulted in a US$81 million loss—a sizable portion of the country's foreign reserves.[1] In 2017, the Shadow Brokers, an appropriately named individual or organization, stole hundreds of megabytes of tools developed by the National Security Agency.[2] Included in the haul was one tool, EternalBlue, that hackers subsequently used in the WannaCry attack that had an impact on over 230,000 computer systems in 150 countries, with costs estimated to be near $4 billion.[3] In 2018, Marriott announced the compromise of its Starwood reservation system, exposing personal and financial information on up to 500 million guests, and India's national ID database Aadhaar (English: Foundation) was hacked, exposing personal, financial, and biometric information for virtually all 1.1 billion citizens in the country.[4]

Obviously, things need to change.

In our experience in consulting with clients across the globe, the core reason why the billions and billions of dollars spent on cybersecurity haven't made a difference to date is that the central focus of cybersecurity has been, and continues to be, on technology—mainly, computers and infrastructure, and their vulnerabilities—instead of the business risks to a company's operations and strategic direction.

Admittedly, there are both historical and logical reasons for why technology has been and continues to be at the center. Computer scientists were the first to look at cybersecurity. They focused on the specific details of attack and defense and how to build the core, or kernel, of the operating systems running computers so they could withstand attack. Of course, without digital technology, cyber risks wouldn't exist, and cybersecurity technologies and the activities surrounding them are important. The focus on fixing computer vulnerabilities is in fact seductively dangerous because there is value involved.

But there are a couple of reasons why this very focus on cybersecurity technology ends up undercutting its capacity to protect. No company has the resources to fix every cybersecurity problem, and not all fixes are equally important. Only by starting with your company's most critical business activities, and how cyberattacks could disrupt them, can you know how to prioritize mitigation of the cyberattacks that can cause them the most harm. Additionally, only when cybersecurity technologists understand how your company conducts business can they avoid making decisions and undertaking activities that, however well intended, don't reduce cyber risks. And, in some cases, they increase the risks while simultaneously interfering with business operations.

Further, the specialized nature of cybersecurity technology, and the jargon-filled language used in describing it, means that nontechnical stakeholders, including boards of directors, don't have a meaningful voice in discussions of how to protect their company from cyber threats. This situation changes when discussions of cyber risk start with protecting both current and strategic activities that generate the most value for your company. This small change in approach puts you and your fellow board members in the right position to oversee the management of cyber risks.

Only by starting with critical business activities, not cybersecurity technologies, will your company know which cybersecurity products to buy and which activities to undertake. The narrow focus on technology also deflects attention from nontechnical dynamics that have much more influence in the effectiveness of the technical cybersecurity products than the sophistication of their features. These dynamics include the motivations, incentives, and priorities of the individuals who maintain and use cybersecurity products or otherwise play a role in your company's cyber defenses. We have encountered many situations, for example, in which employees have deliberately bypassed cybersecurity controls because they interfered with their number-one priority, getting their work done. In other cases, we've seen cybersecurity staff lower cybersecurity product protection levels because of the additional work and pressure if a higher level caused a false alarm or disrupted some aspect of business operations. The effectiveness of the cybersecurity group is influenced by its place within the company structure. If the head of the parent organization has different priorities, the cybersecurity group may not get the funding and visibility it needs.

If your company is ever going to materially improve its cyber defenses, it needs the right catalyst—you and your fellow board members. We view cybersecurity as fundamentally a governance problem and see corporate governance as the most effective approach companies can adopt to address their cybersecurity requirements.

Cybersecurity governance starts at the top, with board of directors' oversight and executives setting management direction. From here, it flows through the rest of the organization, entailing both a shift in responsibility and a shift in focus. Ultimate responsibility for cybersecurity and the management of cyber risk shifts from technology specialists to corporate leadership. Focus shifts from cybersecurity technologies to the business, its operations, strategies, and big bets— and the business risks brought about by cyberattacks that could disrupt or destroy them.

Since you represent the fiduciary interests of your company's owners and are charged with adopting a long-term view of the company's health, profitability, and growth, you have the authority to instigate improvements to overall cybersecurity strategy and cyber defenses. You can step in where market forces have faltered and government regulations won't help.

Digital Stewardship

Many directors have told us that cybersecurity is daunting, if not overwhelming. They feel as if they're making investment decisions without reliable data and don't fully understand the capabilities of cybersecurity technologies. Further, many think that the learning curve is too steep. Others say they don't know what questions to ask about cybersecurity and cyber risk—or what constitutes a good answer. Often, they are left to rely on broad statements from cybersecurity or IT management along the lines of "We're OK over here, but need work over there." Technology-knowledgeable management might have cybersecurity covered, but the suspicion lingers that they may not.

It doesn't have to be this way. You can make improvements simply by fulfilling your governance and oversight duties. Cybersecurity oversight is similar in concept to the "observer effect" in quantum physics, where the observation of an event changes its outcome. Your requests for information motivate your company to pay attention to relevant dynamics and perform necessary analyses that it would not have done otherwise.

Your assumption of cybersecurity responsibility need not be an arduous burden. In spite of the general perception that cybersecurity is complex and impenetrable, our experience shows that its governance and oversight do not require an extensive technical background. While an increased understanding of cybersecurity issues is clearly important, you don't need a deep understanding of cybersecurity to lead your company. Pursuing a formal cybersecurity education would provide limited benefits, and be time-consuming and impractical. In the natural course of your board activities, you will gain the needed familiarity with cybersecurity issues.

To assist you, we have developed a framework called "digital stewardship," which comprises four principles, three responsibilities, and a collection of aide-mémoires. The principles provide concise points of reference to guide you in your cybersecurity deliberation and decision making. The three responsibilities address your company's most important cybersecurity undertakings and give you the foundation for oversight. The aide-mémoires contain a series of inquiries you can use immediately to guide your oversight of these responsibilities. By adopting the digital stewardship framework, you will know how to be a cybersecurity leader, what you should ask of your company, and how to understand and interpret the information it provides you.

The Principles

- *If you don't understand it, they didn't explain it.* Cybersecurity management and staff within a company *are responsible for providing* their board of directors with materials and briefings that nonspecialists can understand.

- *It is the business at risk.* All discussions and actions relating to cybersecurity and cyber risks start and end with the business and the risks to its operations and strategic direction, not with computers and their vulnerabilities.

- *Make cybersecurity mainstream.* In both corporate organization and activities, take cybersecurity from siloed functions and incorporate it into mainstream operations.

- *Engage motivation.* Understand and align the interests and motivations of staff and departments to incentivize behavior that leads to accomplishing cybersecurity goals.

The Responsibilities

Manage Cyber Risks

The most significant cybersecurity responsibility is the management of cyber risk. All other responsibilities both support cyber risk management and depend on a clear understanding of the business impact of cyber incidents. Effectively managing cyber risks requires that you clearly understand the relationships among the most significant business risks a company faces, the types of cyberattacks that could cause these risks, and the mitigating controls to prevent or minimize their impact. Ensuring the effectiveness of the controls includes recognizing and accounting for the nontechnical dynamics that can negate even the most powerful technologies.

Fortify the Company

Companies can substantially improve the overall effectiveness of their cybersecurity activities by utilizing the tools of organizational structure, processes, and culture, while accounting for employee motivations and incentives. The process of discovering new cyber risks will answer the questions, "How secure are we now?" and "How secure will we be tomorrow?" The placement of the cybersecurity group and an understanding of the cyber expertise that boards need—and don't need—can improve the effectiveness of both. Further, a shift in thinking about accountability can unlock valuable information that is essential for informed board and executive decision making.

Lead in Crisis

While a company should not neglect preventative and defensive measures, it needs to be ready for a cyberattack-induced crisis. This readiness entails prior planning, preparation, and coordination in two distinct but related areas. First, a company needs the capacity to recognize and respond to cyberattacks, which includes a skilled cyber response team and the procedures it should follow. Second, the executive team must prepare to lead the company during a cyber crisis, which includes how to treat the situations it will face and what decisions it will make during a crisis. By using information and materials already developed in the process of cyber risk mitigation, executives can think about their course of action before a cyber crisis hits.

Aide-Mémoires

Each of the aide-mémoires in the book has four components. The first part is an inquiry relating to one aspect of your company's cybersecurity responsibilities. We have drafted the inquiries so you can use them directly as written. The second component gives a brief rationale of the inquiry in terms of your company's cyber defenses and cyber risk management activities. The next component gives examples and descriptions of the types of evidence that respond to the inquiry. The final component describes the actions you should take to fulfill your oversight responsibilities relating to the inquiry. Use of the aide-mémoires does not require that you have any prior cybersecurity or technical experience. Further, the aides are effectively key performance indicators for your company's management of cybersecurity and cyber risk.

Guide to the Book

We have written this book specifically to provide counsel and assistance to you, a board member, in fulfilling your cybersecurity governance oversight responsibilities. Given that fulfilling these responsibilities requires your company's input and action, we provide guidance to executive leadership and cybersecurity management both on the cyber protection of their companies and on fulfilling their own responsibilities to you and the board. While specifically addressing corporate boards of directors, the principles and practical guidance we offer here also apply to other types of organizations, including governmental agencies and nonprofits.

The book is divided into four major parts, each contributing to your understanding of cybersecurity in the context of your board oversight responsibilities.

- The first part, "The Problems," lays bare many of the reasons cybersecurity activities don't deliver on their promises and cybersecurity appears so impenetrable. These insights equip you to critically question the rationales for the cybersecurity decisions your company makes.

- The next part includes the four principles of digital stewardship, which are a shorthand guide for all your cybersecurity decisions, especially as you face new and unexpected issues.

- The third part addresses three foundational cybersecurity responsibilities that your company needs to fulfill and you must oversee. Each responsibility addresses the critical and often over-looked factors necessary for success.

- The final part, the aide-mémoires, includes detailed inquiries you can use to gain the necessary assurance that your company is meeting its responsibilities.

Throughout the book, we use examples from the public domain and our own practice to illustrate the application of digital stewardship principles and practices in real life, and some of the consequences when they were not applied.

PART ONE

The Problems

Let's start with two questions:

- Have you ever felt that some of the information you've been told about cybersecurity and cyber risk didn't ring true, but you weren't sure how to articulate this doubt?

- Have you ever suspected that discussions about cybersecurity are more complicated than they need to be?

If so, your intuition is correct. A significant disparity exists between what appears to be true in the area of cybersecurity and what really is. Before addressing digital stewardship principles and responsibilities, we will pull back the curtain on some of the misleading platitudes, hidden dynamics, and misguided voices that give rise to your suspicions and make addressing cybersecurity harder than it must be.

1

Misleading Platitudes

Cybersecurity discourse is full of platitudes that seem obvious and compelling at first, but more thoughtful consideration shows they are misinformed, ineffectual, or counterproductive. Unfortunately, people repeat these platitudes so frequently they take on the patina of truth and distort perceptions about cybersecurity priorities and courses of action. Three such staples of cybersecurity conventional wisdom—"it's a people problem," "protect the crown jewels," and "cyber threats are new and constantly changing"—are especially troubling.

It's a People Problem

"Cybersecurity is a people problem, not a technology problem." This platitude often takes another form: "People are the weakest link." While people do make mistakes, such as losing USB drives and opening malicious email attachments, we don't believe the problem lies with careless employees; rather, the problem rests on cybersecurity staff who fail to address how people behave in the digital world and whose motivations and incentives poorly influence their approaches to protection.

To provide context, compare how we address the people problem when securing the physical world versus the digital world. In the physical world, we understand that certain environments and situations have a higher level of inherent risk, and that people are not always careful when navigating these risks. To compensate, we build in protections to help mitigate the potential harm. These include, for example, putting guardrails on highways and speed bumps in front of schools. We take human behavior into account and don't blame people for, well, being human. We don't think or expect people will act differently just because we tell them to. The situation is radically different in the digital world, where we seldom protect people from making understandable mistakes. Instead, we blame them when they err and recommend more security awareness training as the solution.

Losing USBs

In 2007 and 2008, there were nine incidents in which personal and medical digital information on sixteen thousand Hong Kong residents was accidentally lost. As a result, the Hong Kong Hospital Authority hired us to be part of a task force on patient data security and privacy. Our goal was to understand the root causes for the breaches and recommend security improvements.[1]

One incident involved a clerical staff member at the Prince of Wales Hospital in Hong Kong's New Territories who lost a USB flash drive in a taxi. It would be easy to jump to the conclusion that the staff member's lack of security awareness was the root cause of the incident, just as, in the beginning of a movie or TV show, we might assume that the gun-wielding person standing over a dead body is the murderer.

But we asked only two questions to find out the real root cause: "What do you do at work?" The clerk prepared spreadsheets for interhospital, cross-charge billing for pathology tests performed at Prince of Wales Hospital. "Why did you copy this information onto a USB drive?" The reason wasn't sinister but, instead, a practical frustration many people who work at large companies might face. She didn't have Excel installed on her computer, so she used a USB drive to copy the spreadsheets she got from other hospitals to a colleague's computer that did have Excel so she could do her work. To no avail, she had repeatedly asked IT to install Excel on her computer.

So, this incident was the result of a people problem, but not a problem with the clerk. The problem was with the IT staff who didn't install Excel on her computer. When they eventually installed Excel, the risk of her losing patient information on a USB drive disappeared because she no longer had any reason to use one. This example shows that people are motivated to do their jobs, even if it entails undermining cybersecurity. The clerk was not conscious of the fact that her actions could compromise patient information. She just wanted to do her job.

Phishing

People often open attachments and click on links in emails that result in malware being downloaded onto their computers. Attackers have become savvier in using information gleaned from social media and professional networking sites in crafting these phishing emails, so recipients find it increasingly difficult to tell the difference. While a few Nigerian princes still want to give you millions, their emails have largely been replaced by a variety of more-convincing ones. The University of California at Berkeley keeps a database of phishing attack examples, such as one purporting to be from the human resources department (see figure 1-1).[2]

FIGURE 1-1

Example of phishing attack

From: "HR@berkeley.edu" <HR@berkeley.edu>
Subject: Message from human resources
Date: April 13, 2017 at 9:29:54 PM PDT
To: XXXXX@berkeley.edu

Dear XXXXX@berkeley.edu

An information document has been sent to you by the Human Resources Department.

Click here to Login to view the document. Thank you!

Berkeley University Of California HR Department.
@2017 The Regents of the University of California. All rights reserved.

CONFIDENTIALITY NOTICE: This email and any attachments may contain confidential
information that is protected by law and is for the sole use of the individuals or entities to
which it is addressed. If you are not the intended recipient, please destroying all copies
of the communication and attachments. Further use, disclosure, copying, distribution of,
or reliance upon the contents of this email and attachments is strictly prohibited.

The email in the figure looks legitimate, and the instruction to log
on to your account to view the document isn't suspicious because this
is standard practice for many organizations, especially when a document contains sensitive information. The security advice the Berkeley
Information Security Office offered for this type of example is that
the email recipient should first verify that the link is legitimate before
clicking on it. To perform the verification, the email recipient needs
first to position his or mouse over "Click here" so that the website's
address will appear. Then, most critically, the recipient needs to dis-
cern if it is really the address of the HR department website as opposed
to one trying to impersonate the website.

This advice, with which most cybersecurity experts would agree,
fails to consider two factors. The first is that reading email at work is
not a leisure activity; people try to get through it as quickly as possible.
Many will find that the time to position a mouse over a link, look at a
website address, and decide if it is legitimate or not will take too long.

The other and more important factor is that determining the validity of a website address is not a responsibility that most people can reliably fulfill, so not one that a company should impose on them.

Security Awareness Training

A commonly used control to prevent phishing attacks and, more broadly, the introduction of malicious software into a corporate environment is security awareness training. However, even employees at cybersecurity companies have difficulties internalizing cybersecurity awareness training. Intel Security (formerly McAfee) tested 19,000 people from 140 countries and only 3 percent were able to identify all the phishing emails in a sample of 10, and 80 percent failed to spot any of the phishing emails.[3] No amount of security awareness training can satisfactorily mitigate this risk, as it takes only one person to click on the wrong link or open a tainted attachment in order for this type of attack to succeed.

Identifying Malicious Software

Another tool for foiling phishing attacks, and their associated malware, is anti-malware technologies that work by detecting malicious software before it can establish a beachhead on a computer and start its process of exploitation. Therein lies the problem—how to identify malicious software. Initially, this was done by compiling a list of the signatures, or fingerprints, of known malicious software and comparing it with any new program before allowing the software to run. More-sophisticated anti-malware products look at additional characteristics, including behavior, of potentially malicious software. However, the challenge remains, as defenders constantly try to catch up with the new versions of malicious software that attackers are adept at creating.

In late 2017, the company Malwarebytes, itself a provider of anti-malware solutions, examined malware detection rates from almost 10 million computers and found that even highly ranked anti-malware products failed to detect over 60 percent of the malware it tested.[4] Going back to 2013, the *New York Times* revealed its corporate network had been breached in an attempt to discover reporters' sources.[5] This attack included the use of forty-five different kinds of malicious software, of which only one was detected by its anti-malware solution.

Going further back to the beginnings of computer viruses, the inherent limitations of antivirus solutions were recognized by a founder of the antivirus industry. When the first computer virus appeared in 1986, within two years, there were as many as forty antivirus vendors in this booming market.[6] With this rapid proliferation of vendors, John McAfee, who developed the first successful commercial antivirus program, estimated that "as many as 75% of the products currently being marketed are ineffective in that they do not detect or protect against a significant percent of the viruses."[7] He publicly worried that a "lack of understanding on the part of end users has created an environment conducive to misinformation, emotionalism and fraud."[8] As of 2018, the worldwide annual revenue for these types of products exceeded US$15 billion and was expected to continue to grow at a brisk 10 percent CAGR.[9]

There is an elegant technological solution for addressing phishing attacks and all other types of malicious software that is inherently effective and doesn't require all your employees to make the right decision all the time about what they click on or open. "Application whitelisting" is based on the principle that if malicious software can't run on a computer, it can't harm the computer. It borrows from a practice often used to restrict access to clubs, parties, and other special events—the guest list. Instead of trying to determine if every program or piece of software is malicious, application whitelisting focuses on only allowing software that is already known to be safe to run on a computer. It doesn't matter what links people click on or what attachments they open. It doesn't matter how many new variants of malicious software are created every day. If the malware isn't on the guest list, it won't be let in.

IT Staff Incentives

The security concepts behind application whitelisting have been known for years. There are commercial whitelisting products, and even the Windows and macOS operating systems contain application whitelisting tools. So, the question remains, why aren't people using application whitelisting more broadly? Further, why is it likely that you have never heard of it, while antivirus or anti-malware products are quite familiar? The answer comes down to motivation and blame.

Since current malware defenses aren't effective, infections are routine and perceived as inevitable. When infections do occur, companies blame neither the providers of security awareness training nor the anti-malware solutions for the failure of the products and services. Nor do they blame the staff people who procured these products and services. There is no motivation for the cybersecurity function within an organization to change from approaches that aren't effective to one that is.

There are, however, distinct disincentives for individuals in cybersecurity or IT departments to adopt application whitelisting in lieu of anti-malware. Within a traditional corporate office environment, the deployment of an anti-malware solution is simple, and ongoing management is largely automated. Again, there is no blame if it doesn't work, so long as it is in place. The deployment of an application whitelisting solution requires more effort and attention on the part of IT staff. They need to make sure that updates to existing applications remain on the whitelist and that new, authorized business applications are added. If they don't do this work correctly, and someone in the company can't use their computer or an application they need as a result, the IT staff will be blamed and under great pressure to fix the problem immediately.

The fundamental issue boils down to the question of who has responsibility for creating a safe digital environment in which people can work. To date, companies have largely placed this responsibility on individuals who are in no position to protect themselves, and on technologies that can never be effective. The underlying reasons for this course of action directly relate to incentives and accountability or, more precisely, the lack of it. The platitude "it's a people problem" only serves to mask the issue.

Protect the Crown Jewels

Perhaps the most common type of reported cyber breach is loss of personal information, including financial data, medical information, credit card details, national identity numbers, and passwords, because of attacks on corporate and government computer systems. Close behind are losses of trade secrets, intellectual property, strategic plans, and internal financials. Given that not all digitized assets are of equal worth, it makes sense to prioritize the protection of the most valuable. The problem with the platitude "protect the crown jewels" is that it often promotes activities that are neither appropriate nor effective in reducing a company's most significant cyber risks.

The directive to protect the crown jewels implicitly places the greatest priority on the confidentiality of information. The thinking goes that it's better to delay the speed or convenience of sending or sharing information in order to make sure it doesn't fall into the wrong hands.

However, depending on your specific business or needs, data confidentiality may not be your number-one priority.

For example, if your company operates a multiplayer online game, the necessary computing power and network bandwidth are of utmost priority since you want your games to be available to your hundreds of thousands of gamers whenever they want to play. If they can't play, you'll quickly go out of business.

If your company uses industrial control systems that drive, for example, oil refining, chemical manufacturing, or electric power generation, then speed of communications is critical. These systems comprise many individual computers, often quite old, that are quite sensitive to delays in network communications. If one machine doesn't get a message from another machine when expected, it can malfunction, causing a cascading effect throughout other components of the industrial control system that could result in disruption to or the complete halt of operations.

Speed can also be critical in medical settings. Although cybersecurity priorities in health care tend to center on confidentiality, cybersecurity priorities are flipped upside down in emergency situations. When a patient is in the emergency room or on the operating table, doctors want to get as much patient medical history information available, as quickly as possible. Lives depend on it. During the fog of surgery, if someone gets access to information they shouldn't have, that can be investigated and resolved when the patient is recovering.

These examples show, however, that companies face many other cyber risks unrelated to confidentiality. A focus on protecting crown jewels will not help you in identifying and mitigating these risks. Nor will this approach necessarily provide the comprehensive protection your confidential information needs. This is because many attempts at protecting crown jewels focus on protecting information where it is stored. Hence, the common post-breach question, Was the data encrypted? This question usually refers to the primary database where the information is stored. However, in order for information to provide value, it has to be taken out of the database, shared, and used. The risk exposure is much greater during these activities than when the information is resting in a database. To address the goals of prioritizing cybersecurity attention and providing complete protection, your company should focus on protecting its most important business activities, and you'll get the protection of sensitive information as part of the process.

Take, for example, customer service for accounts and billing. This business activity requires access to sensitive personal information, such as addresses and ID numbers, and sensitive financial information, such as credit card and bank account numbers. By tracing the process of creating a new customer account to customer service interactions while the account is active, to the closing of the account, your company will know all the computers where this information is stored, all the computer networks the information traverses, and all the individuals and organizations who have access. Your company needs to protect not only sensitive customer information but, more broadly, your customers' trust.

An additional benefit of focusing on critical business activities is that you may identify types of information you previously didn't realize were so critical. The relatively low-tech business of growing and selling almonds, walnuts, and pistachios in California's Central Valley provides a case in point. Nuts are an attractive target for thieves. One truckload of nuts can be worth up to US$500,000 and, unlike electronic equipment, the nuts have no serial numbers. Once eaten, the evidence is gone. Innovative thieves have moved beyond hijacking trucks on lonely stretches of road in favor of cyber-based attacks. They start by hacking into nut growers' and processors' computers to steal information about planned shipments. This allows them to generate legitimate-looking paperwork for already scheduled shipments and then send their own trucks before the real drivers arrive. In some cases, the thieves hire drivers who are unaware that they are participating in a robbery.[10]

A characteristic that "protect the crown jewels" shares with other cybersecurity platitudes is that it makes it easy for people to think that they already understand a problem and know how to solve it. This discourages them from examining cybersecurity problems more thoroughly and therefore finding better and more effective solutions.

Cyber Threats Are New and Constantly Changing

Because companies are overwhelmed by the seemingly ever-increasing number of new cyber threats, they make two common mistakes. They think that investment in protection should be proportionate to the size of the threat. If the threat is increasing dramatically, so should the investment. In a similar vein, they think they need to make more investment to combat a threat never seen before. Given that these perceptions of urgency influence cybersecurity investment decisions, it's useful to explore them more thoroughly.

How Fast the World Turns Depends on Where You Stand

The rapid changes in the cyber threat landscape are an oft-quoted reason for boards of directors' more frequent briefings on cybersecurity. While we fully agree that cybersecurity warrants more time on your agenda, it is because of the breadth and importance of the topic, not its pace of change.

One metric commonly used to indicate the rapid growth of cyber threats is the volume of new malware. Numbers for 2017 range from

15,107,232 to 128,160,000, and that only accounts for the malicious software that anti-malware vendors were able to detect.[11] While these numbers are large, they are also largely meaningless. There is no real difference between how a company protects itself from a million types of malware versus 10 million or 100 million. The real issue is how to neutralize any malware.

If You Don't Know It, It's New to You

The relative recentness of broad cybersecurity awareness contributes to the perception that the cyber threats we are facing are new. Yet the cybersecurity field can trace its roots back more than five decades to the 1960s when the US Air Force was concerned about something that now fills headlines as a new threat: nation-state attacks on critical infrastructure. The nation-state in question was the Soviet Union, and the critical infrastructure was the US nuclear arsenal. The specific risk—use of malware to compromise computer systems—seems strangely contemporary as well. A preeminent concern at that time, according to (Ret.) Air Force Colonel Roger Schell, who was intimately involved in these matters, was that malware in the computers controlling the navigation of land-based nuclear missiles could redirect these missiles to attack US cities.[12]

Given that internet connectivity in the 1960s was nothing like what we have today, the primary methods for infecting computers with malware were software developers and the tools to turn the programs they wrote into instructions that machines could understand. To address these risks, developers underwent background investigations, and all their tools were developed in-house. While the economics of software development have changed over the years, a risk cybersecurity experts understood in the 1960s reappeared in 2015.

Apple provides a tool named Xcode for programmers who are developing applications for iOS devices, such as iPhones and iPads. While Apple provides this tool for free, it can also be downloaded from websites catering to software developers. One of these sites, Baidu Yunpan, contained a malware version of Xcode, called XcodeGhost, that added extra instructions into programs without the knowledge of the software developer.[13] These instructions, when incorporated into popular applications downloaded tens of millions of times, could steal personal information from the users of the applications and send it to an unknown server.

Beyond the insight that the US Air Force recognized this type of cyberattack fifty years earlier, the broader lesson for companies is the importance of understanding just what and whom they are depending on for protection against cyber threats. Companies do not ask this question nearly enough, and you are ideally positioned to correct this situation.

In the winter of 1970, the US Defense Science Board Task Force on Computer Security published a report entitled "Security Controls for Computer Systems."[14] Commonly referred to as the Ware Report after its primary author Willis Ware, it identified a majority of cyber vulnerabilities and risks that we still face today, a sample of which we summarize in table 1-1.

TABLE 1-1

Sample of ongoing cyber vulnerabilities

Topic area	Specific concern	Relevance today
Files	Theft, copying, and unauthorized access to sensitive information	This is still one of the most significant cyber risks organizations face.
Software	Failure of protection features, including control over what information people can access	In most cases of insider theft of company information, a failure of access controls facilitated the theft.

(Continued)

TABLE 1-1

Sample of ongoing cyber vulnerabilities (*Continued*)

Topic area	Specific concern	Relevance today
Users	Weak authentication of computer users	Criminals impersonating users, often through the use of stolen passwords, continue to haunt both companies and individuals.
Network communications	Ability to tap and intercept network traffic	The risk still exists, but fortunately encryption solutions are widely deployed.
System administration	Administration mistakes resulting in compromise	One of the major risks of the internet of things and the expanding adoption of technologies outside IT department control is that the users of these devices do not know how to manage them securely. In addition, many of the breaches of corporate information stored in the cloud are due to configuration mistakes.
Programmers	Programmers modifying their software to disable security features introduce back doors and otherwise subvert security	All these concerns currently exist.

The fundamental cyber vulnerabilities computers face are neither growing nor new. The innovative ways in which we are using and combining digital technologies introduce new challenges, but these are all variations on existing themes.

Further, although computers now come in a variety of packages ranging from mainframes and laptops to watches and refrigerators, and require new approaches for protection, the cybersecurity issues are fundamentally the same. In a similar vein, so are the attacks. Certain particulars of an attack may be different, but the attack is not fundamentally different. Think, for example, of emails containing links that, when clicked, result in the download of malicious software onto your laptop. Now think of an SMS that, when clicked, results in the download of malicious software onto your phone. The delivery mechanisms are different, email versus SMS, and the malicious software will be different to accommodate running on a laptop versus a phone, but they are the same cyberattack. This situation is analogous to a store that claims to have forty different shirts, but in reality, it is selling one shirt in four sizes and ten colors.

In this chapter, we showed how common cybersecurity platitudes draw our attention from what really is important to what only seems to be. In the next chapter, we show how dynamics that are just out of sight expose commonly accepted truths about cyber defenses.

2

Hidden Dynamics

Effective cybersecurity requires awareness of a host of nontechnical factors, or hidden dynamics. These dynamics are not lines of code or circuits etched into silicon that only engineers and programmers can comprehend. Rather, they're business factors that you already know but might not have associated with cybersecurity.

First, we address the dynamic we call the "chimera of compliance"—the inherent limitations of cybersecurity standards and the regulations based on them as a way to determine a company's cybersecurity posture. Next, we look at the second dynamic, "employee motivation"—how employees simply trying to excel at their jobs can engage in behavior that creates new cyber risks for their company. Then we examine the "economics of cyberattack"—the financial incentives of the cyberattack tools and services market and raise the question, "Does it really matter who attacked us?" Finally we look at the "asymmetry of attack and defense"—the relationship between the power of an attack and the required strength of the defense, and how the cyber dynamics are completely different from what we are accustomed to in a traditional battle.

Chimera of Compliance

When you engage in cybersecurity, one of your first areas of interest is understanding how well your company is protected against cyberattack. Questions such as "How safe are we?" "Are we doing the right things?" "Are we doing enough?" are typical. In lieu of undertaking business-oriented cyber-risk assessments—which we will discuss later in the book—to answer these questions, companies often use compliance with cybersecurity standards to judge their level of protectiveness and to prioritize future investments. Although cybersecurity standards can provide you with useful ideas on common issues, in order to derive value from these standards, you need to understand their purpose, limits, and the unintended consequences of having to comply with multiple standards and regulations.

Inherent Limitations of Standards

Apply to All and None

Cybersecurity standards, by design, address broad audiences. One metric of a standard's success is the scale of its adoption. However, in attempting to speak to everyone, cybersecurity standards address the needs of no one specifically. The NIST Framework for Improving Critical Infrastructure Cybersecurity (commonly referred to as the NIST Framework) was originally developed to help reduce cyber risks to critical infrastructure.[1] However, the introduction to the framework clearly states that any company or organization can use the standard, and companies in industries as varied as retail and hospitality are increasingly adopting it. The cybersecurity priorities for a nuclear power plant are clearly different from those of a department store or hotel. No standard, regardless of how well drafted, can provide specific guidance to such a disparate collection of organizations.

Even having a cybersecurity standard issued by your own industry association doesn't guarantee that it provides helpful and specific guidance pertaining to your industry. For example, the American Chemistry Council published its "Implementation Guide for Responsible Care Security Code of Management Practices."[2] While arguably this guide provides helpful advice on cybersecurity management practices, there is nothing that specifically addresses the unique cybersecurity challenges within the industrial control systems that drive chemical manufacturing. It is sufficiently generic that it applies equally to the IT systems within the corporate front office of a chemical company and to the manufacturing systems for which it was written.

To address the lack of standards, many companies develop their own policies. This is a smart move, but you need to make sure that your own standards, unlike industry and external standards, are specific to your business. And you need to keep up with growth. If you acquire companies and build new products, your cybersecurity approaches will need to change. For example, a financial services client developed its cybersecurity standard when it relied on the computing power of scores of mainframes housed in its own data centers. This served it well for a long time. However, as market conditions evolved, its services changed, as did its method of delivery. Its standard became increasingly irrelevant.

This irrelevance became particularly important when the firm bought an Indian company whose transaction processing was hosted by a cloud provider. The first issue was that the existing cybersecurity standard couldn't give any guidance on what it should do to protect itself from the cyber risks faced. The second was that it was perennially noncompliant with the corporate standard and management had to spend significant and unproductive time dealing with the inevitable audit findings.

Always Out-of-Date

Cybersecurity standards are always out-of-date. For example, one of the best-known international cybersecurity standards, ISO 27001, was first published in 2005.[3] It took eight years for a revision. In 2018, the North American Electric Reliability Corporation promulgated its Critical Infrastructure Protection (CIP) standard, version 5. This standard replaces its urgent action standard 1200 that was first approved fifteen years earlier, in 2003.[4]

The issue is not that the standards can't keep up with rapidly changing cyber threats. In chapter 1, we explained how this rapid change is overstated. The issue is that the standards can't keep up with the rapid pace of business. Changes in business operations and changes in services offered and products produced account for the new cyber risks that businesses face.

Financial Incentives

The process of certifying compliance with a cybersecurity standard demonstrates how financial incentives affecting both the auditor and the audited can question the meaningfulness of a particular compliance. Companies usually pay external auditors who then vouch for their compliance with regulations and industry standards, thereby introducing potential conflicts and blind spots. The Payment Card Industry Data Security Standard (PCI DSS) provides a good case study.[5]

Shortly after publication of the initial PCI DSS in 2004, we set up a Qualified Security Assessors (QSA) practice in Asia to perform credit card security assessments. One of the first things we noticed was that the primary motivation for most merchants, and other companies that store or process payment card information, was not protection of credit card information. It was getting the annual report on compliance that showed they were, indeed, compliant. In addition, clients wanted to get the report at the lowest possible price with the least amount of effort.

Even in our work for one of the founding PCI payment brands, the low cost of assessment was such a priority that we stopped working with it. It was impossible to hire qualified assessors at the price it was willing to pay.

On the other hand, the companies and individuals that perform compliance assessments are motivated to maximize income and profit. It is a business after all. The QSA company can accomplish this most easily through repeat business, as PCI DSS audits are an annual event. However, a QSA is unlikely to be hired next year if it gives a client a failing grade this year. Many individual QSA assessors we've talked to said their management often reminded them about this business reality.

Another factor affecting the quality of a PCI assessment is the amount of time spent on it. For the individual QSA, performing more and more assessments can have a significant impact on its total compensation. Trustwave is the largest QSA; one of its former assessors said, "The more assessments you could cram into a quarter, the bigger and juicier your bonus was going to be." An employee with a base salary of $100,000, for instance, could generate $30,000 to $50,000 more a year by churning out as many assessment reports as possible.[6]

The protection of credit card information is clearly important, and PCI assessments are one means of increasing this protection. However, nontechnical dynamics, such as the financial motivations we just described, diminish the value of the assessments. Home Depot, for example, was PCI-compliant at the time it suffered a breach that compromised 56 million of its customers' credit cards details.[7]

Compliant versus Protected

The proliferation of new cybersecurity regulations has some positive results: companies are doing more to protect their assets and their customers. But the regulations have unintended consequences. Because of the sheer number of regulations and the burden of complying with them, companies are losing sight of the most significant cyber risks.

There are several issues at play. The first, as the example of Home Depot illustrates, is that compliance with a cybersecurity standard is not the same as being protected. Determining what constitutes sufficient cyber protection is a different and larger undertaking than meeting the requirements of a regulation. The second issue relates to how people deal differently with immediate pain versus future pain. Noncompliance with a regulation entails predictable and immediate pain in terms of fines, penalties, and other punitive measures. Corporate compliance departments exist precisely to avoid this pain. On the other hand, neither the impact of a potential cyber breach nor its timing is known. This is a future pain and, while recognized as important, doesn't convey the same urgency for many as regulatory noncompliance does. Therefore, determining real cybersecurity requirements takes a backseat to compliance. A further unintended consequence is that companies more and more think compliance is a proxy for being secure and do not consider additional risk-reduction activities.

Employee Motivation

Employees are motivated to do their jobs and do them well. Their desire for a promotion, a bonus, or a manager's approval, or the feeling of being a productive member of a team, are all factors that can drive this motivation. Here's the problem. Unless employees work in a company's cybersecurity department, their motivation and incentives have nothing to do with cybersecurity. Most employees are cybersecurity agnostic. They don't want their companies to suffer a cyber breach and don't want to contribute to such a breach. But, given the proper motivation, employees *will* act in ways that can compromise your company's cybersecurity.

Get the Job Done

One example of this dynamic comes from an Asian automobile manufacturer that suffered a US$1 billion loss because of an unpublicized cyber breach that compromised advanced R&D information. After the breach, senior executives directed the IT cybersecurity team to improve the protection of information relating to its development of new automobiles. The approach the cybersecurity team took was to embed the network used for automotive design within the corporate intranet. The rationale was that an external attacker would have to breach two networks instead of one to steal the company's sensitive information. This borrows from European medieval castle protection practices that included both a moat and a wall.

Unfortunately, the cybersecurity team did not understand the process of designing a car; the design team worked closely with external partners that needed to access and share the same information. By walling off the auto design network, the cybersecurity team blocked access to these external partners and, as a result, rendered the company's own employees unproductive. So what did the employees do? They created fake employee accounts for their partners to access the information on the company's intranet. None of the employees felt the need to tell anyone about what they were doing.

Later, when we asked them if they understood that their actions exposed the company to increased cyber risk, they said yes. But they weren't really apologizing. Since their job is to design cars, they didn't think twice about removing an obstacle that was preventing them from moving forward. They were only concerned about the immediacy of the situation, in which they needed to get work done, and the certainty of the consequences—they'd miss a deadline.

The increased cyber exposure that resulted from their actions was uncertain. Their external partners may or may not abuse their insider access. And if they do, it could be tomorrow, next month, next year, or beyond. Further, the employees are unlikely to hear about any abuse, even if it happens.

Cybersecurity Disincentives

Financial incentives can exacerbate the potential conflict between an employee doing a job and a company protecting itself. These incentives are tied either to individual accomplishments, such as meeting a stretch goal, or to department achievements, such as meeting a milestone. Take, for example, a new product release or corporate acquisition. Both activities should include a number of different cybersecurity tasks. For a new product, the company should select, implement, and test the right set of security features. For a corporate acquisition, the company should analyze the target company's cybersecurity posture to support accurate pricing of the deal. But if performing these security tasks, or performing them well, delays the release or deal closure, cyber-risk reduction will take a backseat. Employees and executives get bonuses for meeting deadlines; they don't get bonuses for missing a deadline, even if the reason is to prevent a downstream cyber incident whose impact would far eclipse that of launching a product a couple of weeks or months late.

The Samsung Galaxy Note 7 is a case in point. The phone's penchant for spontaneous combustion, covered extensively in the media, wasn't the result of cyber vulnerabilities; rather, it was a mix of culture and incentives that put schedule ahead of safety. In hopes of exploiting a lackluster Apple iPhone release cycle, Samsung accelerated its production schedule, rushing a feature-rich product saddled with latent design and manufacturing defects to market.[8] In the aftermath, Samsung lost approximately US$9.5 billion in sales and US$5 billion in profit, instead of gaining the competitive advantage it had hoped for.[9]

Economics of Cyberattack

Knowing the capabilities of potential adversaries has long been a staple of statecraft; this carries over to the digital world. The technical sophistication of cyber adversaries, especially nation-states, frequently factor into the selection of cyber defenses. A combination of market forces and technology is challenging some long-held assumptions in this area and is rendering the question "Who done it?" less relevant. These changes have a direct impact on cybersecurity investment as well as on the overall approach to assessing cyber risks.

National Capabilities

Many believe that certain cyber superpowers, such as North Korea, Russia, China, and the United States, have the necessary technical capabilities and resources to build sophisticated hacking tools beyond the reach of anyone else. This assumption is used both as a rationale for increased cybersecurity funding, and as an excuse when cybersecurity defenses fail. While it still takes a well-financed and technically sophisticated country to field an aircraft carrier, the same is not true to develop cyberattack tools.

For example, two security researchers, Brian Meixell and Dillon Beresford, armed only with MacBook Pro laptops and no investment beyond their time, were able to demonstrate how they "could penetrate even the most heavily fortified facilities in the world, without the backing of a nation state."[10] They did this by exploiting a flaw in programmable logic controllers (PLCs) from a prominent manufacturer.

PLCs are the workhorses of industrial automation. They control everything from robots on a factory floor to machinery in oil refineries and centrifuges in nuclear power plants. As is true of so many technologies and products, they were developed without considering cybersecurity, and as a result, the communications between PLCs are not always encrypted. This flaw enabled Meixell and Beresford to send specially crafted messages to a PLC with the result that they took complete control over it. They could make it operate incorrectly or not at all. Further, they could use one compromised PLC as a staging point to then take over all the PLCs within an entire industrial control system environment.

The lore of Silicon Valley is full of stories of vastly successful companies with very modest roots. Apple and Hewlett-Packard, for instance, were both literally started in the founders' garages. Perhaps there will be a similar storyline about the most sophisticated cyberattacks, not being developed in the basements of secret government buildings, but rather in hip, urban cafés by people like Meixell and Beresford working on their laptops.

"Nobody but Us" No More

Even if a nation-state develops a sophisticated hacking tool, it doesn't mean that it will retain its use exclusively. With an annual budget exceeding US$10 billion, the US National Security Agency (NSA) has invested heavily in developing an impressive arsenal of hacking tools for its exclusive use.[11] Thanks to a string of embarrassing leaks and hacks, enterprising organizations are now marketing these tools to a global market of eager consumers, who have used them to devastating effect.

The WannaCry ransomware outbreak—still one of the most devastating in cybersecurity history—provides a good example of how nation-states can't always keep their hacking tools to themselves. While governments will continue to hold monopolies on certain capabilities, such as maintaining a standing military, their cyberattack capacities are no longer NOBUS (nobody but us). They are within reach of individuals and organizations, criminal or otherwise.

In a four-day period from May 12 to May 15, 2017, the WannaCry ransomware infected more than 200,000 computers in 150 different countries.[12] Ransomware is one type of malicious software that encrypts the data on an infected computer. Only if the victim pays a ransom will the hacker provide the encryption key to decrypt and therefore regain access to the data.

The NSA's hacking group, Tailored Access Operations, developed the tool that enabled WannaCry, EternalBlue. It was part of a large trove of NSA cyber weapons stolen by the Shadow Brokers, a hacking organization intent on making a commercial market for these cyber weapons to governments, enterprises, and individuals alike. After initially putting EternalBlue up for auction, the Shadow Brokers published it for free in April 2017.[13]

Less than a month after its public release, thousands of companies found themselves affected by WannaCry, sometimes with disastrous results.[14] For many days, Britain's National Health Service was disrupted, and some of its facilities were forced to divert ambulances and turn away noncritical emergencies.[15] Auto manufacturers Honda, Nissan, and Renault each were forced to shut down production lines.[16]

Efficient Markets of Hacking

The broad economics of cyberattacks are changing in a way that puts sophisticated hacking tools and services in the hands of anyone who can pay. And in many cases, the price is surprisingly reasonable. The market has evolved to include a wide variety of tools and services, available not only to governments, but to anyone who can afford the often modest fees. For example, regimes with relatively modest budgets, such as the Democratic Republic of the Congo, the United Arab Emirates, and Zimbabwe, have been able to acquire Verint Systems' SkyLock tool, which allows them to "locate, track [and] manipulate" more than 70 percent of mobile phones anywhere in the world.[17] The addressable market is as large as it is global. Verint, with humble roots as a call-recording solution for call centers, has entered the lucrative market of surveillance tools and cyber weapons, boasting clientele in over 180 countries.[18] Selling cyber weapons is a growth industry. The global retail market for cyber weapons enjoys double-digit growth rates, expanding from nearly zero in 2001 to what is estimated to be a US$20 billion market in 2016.[19]

Furthermore, a sophisticated black market has stepped up to address the demand for what commercial vendors are unwilling or unable to sell.[20] Operating both in dark corners of the internet and in plain sight, a cottage industry of individuals and organizations can peddle their wares and services to a global audience of buyers. It is a competitive and largely frictionless economy, and sellers are adopting customer-focused business models and sales strategies formerly reserved for innovative retailers and well-funded procurement departments. They differentiate themselves with features, such as 24-7 customer support, service guarantees, and warranties. They have adopted innovative pricing models including subscription services, volume discounts, tiered pricing, and comprehensive catalogs of their hacking services and cyber weapons.

Following the successes of organizations like Spotify, Netflix, and Amazon Prime, some enterprising hackers are adopting a subscription model to market their products and services. The Shadow Brokers, the organization behind the NSA leaks and WannaCry, decided in 2017 to launch what it called the "Data Dump of the Month Club." For a reasonable monthly subscription fee, members get access to upcoming leaks, including a typical assortment of zero-day vulnerabilities for operating systems, smartphones, and financial networks, as well as more exotic "network information from Russian, Chinese, Iranian, and North Korean nuclear missile programs."[21]

For those looking for a full-service experience, the rising "hacking as a service" market includes the entire cyberattack value chain, from research and analysis to design, development, and execution, and can be outsourced to a third party. One example is the now-defunct web-stresser.org, a consumer-friendly retailer that, for a nominal fee, would perform denial of service attacks against any company or organization its customers identified. With the promise of great service and "24-7 customer support," it offered a value-based monthly subscription model ranging from $18.99 for the "bronze" option to $49.99 for its "platinum" service.[22]

This market is evolving, efficient, and competitive, and readily connects criminals to the technical tools and talent they need. It democratizes what was formerly the domain of nation-states and sophisticated criminal organizations and makes hacking tools and services available to anyone with money and a mission. No technical expertise necessary. Given these changing dynamics, companies need to focus instead on the value of their information, operations, or even disruption of operations, not just to themselves but to others. How much is an organization or individual willing to spend? It doesn't matter whether it builds, buys, or rents the attack capability. It will make a market.

Asymmetry of Attack and Defense

In traditional warfare going back to the days of shields and spears, there has been a proportional relationship between the power of an attack and the strength of the necessary defense. This relationship continues when comparing, for example, the piercing power of a bunker buster munition and the depth and hardening of the bunker it is intended to bust. In the digital world, this proportional relationship doesn't exist. Defenses against sophisticated cyberattacks can, quite commonly, be simple, inexpensive, and at times routine.

WannaCry

The NSA-developed attack tool powering WannaCry was admittedly sophisticated. Let's now look at what companies could have done or did do proactively so that WannaCry couldn't hold them hostage:

1. Update Windows. We are all accustomed to seeing notifications on our computers and phones that we should install software updates that often fix security vulnerabilities. Microsoft released a security update that neutralized WannaCry around twenty days before it hit the internet. Installing security patches is neither sophisticated nor expensive, and for desktop computers and laptops, it can be done automatically.[23]

2. Back up their systems and data. If a company makes regular and timely backups, then even if WannaCry had infected its computers, it could restore a previous, clean version of its systems and data and get back to work.

There are a couple of interesting lessons we can learn from WannaCry, beyond how it came to be used or how to defend against it. First, failure to protect a company from WannaCry was a management issue, not a technical one. The preventative technology and activities are routine, but there was insufficient priority placed on them. Second, while WannaCry was sophisticated, the information that board members need to understand about this attack is not, and is completely contained within this chapter.

Quantum Insert

Quantum Insert is another example of a cyberattack tool that the NSA developed at significant expense.[24] While it is difficult to put an exact price on Quantum Insert's development cost, the NSA's budget in 2013 included an increase of US$32 million for "unconventional solutions."[25] This tool goes beyond simply eavesdropping on a target's internet browsing to instead using someone's browsing as an opportunity to install malicious software on their computer. Quantum Insert jumps into action when it sees a target request a page on a website. Before the website can respond, the Quantum Insert tool embeds malicious software in a web page and then sends it to the target. Since the target's browser is expecting to receive a page from the website, it accepts the malicious page without question.

This type of tool has been so popular that companies created commercial versions for countries with more modest budgets. For example, Gamma International GmbH sold a similar tool developed by Dreamlab Technologies AG to the government of Turkmenistan for 875,000 Swiss francs (approximately US$858,000).[26] Not to be outdone, China created a comparable tool called the Great Cannon.[27]

The fundamental problem with Quantum Insert and its imitators is the ease with which they can be defeated. They are powerless in the presence of encrypted web browsing because they can't see the details necessary to forge their web page replies. Increasingly, websites support encryption. And these are not just banking and online shopping sites. Even an emoji website—https://emojipedia.org/—encrypts.

You can tell if your communications to a website are encrypted by looking at the first five letters of the address. If they are "https," then the connection is encrypted and you are immune to the attack. This protection is free and doesn't require any action on your part. If you don't want to rely on individual websites for your protection, you can use a virtual private network (VPN) service that encrypts all of your internet communications. There are VPN services that are free or charge a modest fee.

Understanding the lack of proportionality between cyberattack and defense will assist you in two aspects of your oversight responsibilities. The first relates to cybersecurity investments. You recognize the need to challenge any calls for significant new investment based solely on claims of the sophistication of new cyberattacks. Additionally, you know that the sophistication of a cyberattack is not a valid excuse for your company's failure to protect itself.

3

Misguided Voices

Media, advertising, and, to some extent, popular culture influence our awareness and prioritization of cyber risks and how to mitigate them. Since cybersecurity is a relatively new topic of interest, you may not have the context in which to interpret news headlines and determine their relevance for your company or what follow-on questions you should ask. While increased exposure to cybersecurity will make this process easier over time, you'll need to consider additional factors when absorbing cybersecurity news. These include interpreting cybersecurity information and considering the interests and objectives of the source.

Two of the most common commentators on cybersecurity are *governments* and *cybersecurity vendors*. Since most of their messages are conveyed through news media, we'll address characteristics of *media* that influence what cybersecurity stories get covered and what don't.

Governments

A fundamental government responsibility is to provide for the common good. Historically, this has included provision of a national defense, law enforcement, and an economic environment that improves living standards. While differences of opinion remain regarding the details of accomplishing these goals, there is broad agreement that these are important priorities. With increased digitization in all areas of life, governments are evaluating their evolving roles and how best to serve people and companies.

Duty to Warn

Governments often provide warnings of imminent or expected disasters: air raids in London during World War II, hurricanes in the southeast United States, tsunamis in the Indian Ocean. Each of these circumstances shares two characteristics. The first is that the recommended courses of action, for example, go to a bomb shelter, drive away, or move to higher ground, are easily understood. The second is that people can follow these recommendations.

Unfortunately, warnings about cyber threats aren't usually as understandable and actionable. You may remember that, in the spring of 2018, both the United States and the United Kingdom issued an advisory about Russian cyberattacks against governments, businesses, and individuals.[1] The advisories highlighted the threat to network routers, the specialized computers that bring the internet into our homes, as well as internet-connected devices such as thermostats and cameras that fall under the broad category of the internet of things. The advisory stated that it wasn't clear how successful the Russian hackers were or even the intent of such intrusions. The advisory concluded with recommendations for figuring out if your own home network was breached and how to strengthen its defenses against possible future breaches.

The problem was, the proposed recommendations were beyond the comprehension of the very individuals whose devices were under attack. In addition, some of the recommendations, such as negotiating contract provisions with internet service providers, were impossible to accomplish, given the power disparity between consumers and providers.

Around the same time this advisory was issued, the Ministry of Foreign Affairs in the Netherlands issued a letter warning Dutch travelers to Turkey, China, Russia, and Iran of cyber threats to their electronic devices.[2] The recommended precautions, such as bringing "clean" laptops and mobile phones with minimal data, are standard governmental advice for international travel. The problem with this type of advice is that it doesn't consider the information and technology required for people to conduct business while traveling. It further fails to address the practicalities of living and working in a foreign country.

While there may be other, perhaps geopolitical motivations for issuing these warnings, they do not contribute to protecting the businesses and individuals for whom the warnings are ostensibly issued. They instead raise concerns without providing a path to reduce fear.

Should You Accept Government Assistance?

The increasing, successful number of cyberattacks on businesses, often attributed to nation-states, has prompted active discussion of extending governmental national defense responsibilities to protect companies from cyberattack. This proposal has important ramifications for businesses. Traditional national defense benefits from well-defined national borders and (relatively) easily identifiable adversaries. These benefits disappear on the digital battlefield.

The first issue to address is identifying the attacker. This is easy to accomplish before an attack if, for example, a row of tanks is deployed at your border. Not so for a cyberattack that can originate from anywhere in the world. An attack on a company in Boston that appears to be from North Korea could have originated in New York, following a circuitous path through France and Singapore on the way. All the telltale signs typically used to identify cyberattackers, such as the prove-nance of hacking software, the default language of the computer hack-ers use to develop the software, and the addresses of computers they use in the attack, can be easily modified to throw off the scent. Further, all these indicators can only be analyzed after an attack has started. We can't know the foreign origin of a cyberattack in advance, and therefore we can't know the appropriateness of a military response either.

With any governmental offer of direct cyber defense assistance, busi-ness leaders need to consider what risks they can and cannot reduce, and if government help could introduce new risks. Most proposals for military and law enforcement cyber services include monitoring of all the computer network communications entering and leaving a company. This addresses the risk of internet-based attacks using malware. Monitoring cannot, how-ever, address any cyber risks whose mitigation requires an understanding of how a company operates and conducts business. It could not have prevented the billion-dollar loss at the Asian automobile manufacturer described in chapter 2 or, for example, detected financial fraud in a procurement depart-ment or a joint venture partner's theft of intellectual property.

In addition to clues of a cyberattack, monitored communications also contain a treasure trove of a company's sensitive information that is now in the hands of a government. For multinational companies, monitoring could involve more than one government. Given that the global inter-ests of nations and multinational companies are not the same, there is a risk that information a government collects for preventing cyberattacks could be used for other purposes. The global head of security for a mul-tinational mining client declined the offer of security network monitor-ing services from a US government bureau for this very reason.[3] Several years later, the same bureau approached the global head's successor with a similar offer. Hidden in the fine print of the agreement, the bureau stated that it was free to use any information it collected to pursue crim-inal investigations. The global head declined the offer again. Even if this information is never repurposed, it is still at risk while in government care. Government agencies, including the NSA—whose middle name is literally "security"—don't have the best track record in protecting themselves and their information from cyberattacks.[4]

This is not a critique of government intentions to provide cybersecurity assistance. Rather, we highlight that the nature of assistance governments offer is directly related to the types of threats they are accustomed to addressing, such as military aggression from other countries. Businesses face different threats that they need to address according to different priorities.

Cybersecurity Vendors

Although growth of the cybersecurity market outpaces much of the rest of the economy, there is still intense competition. According to one estimate, in 2018 approximately 2,300 cybersecurity vendors were chasing a dozen or so commodity product types.[5] And the number of market entrants is only going to increase. Vendors face great pressure to stand apart from their direct competitors and distinguish their offerings from those that address different cyber risks.

Surveys and Reports

Vendors sometimes use surveys and reports that highlight the enormity of impact or the scale of their capabilities in order to establish uniqueness in a crowded field. Vendors, especially those that aren't well established, can raise awareness by publishing reports on the anticipated cost of cybercrime. Cybersecurity Ventures' 2016 report warned of the coming "hackerpocalyse" in 2021 when it projected that the annual global cost of cybercrime will reach US$6 trillion.[6] To put this number in perspective, it exceeds the nominal GDP of every single country in the world except for the United States and China.

CrowdStrike's annual global threat report provides a different type of example. In addition to collating public information on cyber incidents, its 2018 report included data on 90.1 billion daily events that were collected by its Falcon platform.[7] The network monitoring it performs is like the government-proposed monitoring we described earlier and has the same limitations, if not the same risks. The 90 billion events all relate to the same, single type of internet malware attack. It doesn't address internal cyber risks, such as a disgruntled IT staff person shutting down critical air traffic control systems.

Raising awareness of a company's cybersecurity offerings by mischaracterizing the threat has a long history. In the March 19, 2009, written testimony of AT&T's former senior vice president and chief security officer, Edward Amoroso, before the US Senate Committee on Commerce, Science, and Transportation, Amoroso wrote: "Last year the FBI announced that revenues from cyber-crime, for the first time ever, exceeded drug trafficking as the most lucrative illegal global business, estimated at reaping more than US$1 trillion annually in illicit profits."[8] He provided no supporting reference for the claim. To put the figure in context, the supposed profits would have exceeded those of AT&T itself by a factor of eighty, as well as the GDP of all but twelve countries.[9] Just a few pages later in his testimony, Amoroso suggested that federal procurement priorities should change to encourage civilian agencies to use the anti-denial of service attack services that AT&T provides.[10]

Legislating Demand

Legislating market demand, as Amoroso was suggesting, is another approach to increasing product demand and revenue. In 2017, Israeli mobile phone forensics vendor Cellebrite lobbied for a New York state law that would have required the use of its Textalyzer product to perform forensic analysis of the mobile phones of all drivers involved in an accident to detect if any texting took place before the accident.[11] Within the United States, forty-nine states have "texting while driving" laws on the books, and annually nearly 18,000 state and local law enforcement agencies report 6.3 million motor vehicle crashes.[12] Given the potential size of this market, Cellebrite supports similar legislation in other states and lobbies at the national level as well.[13]

Vendors use these large numbers to attract attention and focus on specific cybersecurity risks and solutions.[14] While many reports that cybersecurity vendors issue have genuinely useful information, you need to consider the highlighted cyber risks in the context of your own company and be suspicious of all estimates of financial damage.

Media

The news media are the primary means through which governments and cybersecurity vendors publicize their messages, so are a primary source of the information that frames our understanding and prioritization of cybersecurity issues. A couple of factors influence the cyber news that is available.

Reporting What Is Known

Obviously, the media can only report on cyberattacks or breaches that they know about and that are already public to some extent. These breaches are made public in several common ways:

- The effects of the breach are visible, as was the case with the 2015 hacking of the Ukrainian electric power grid.[15]

- The hackers themselves publicize the breach, often to highlight the poor cybersecurity hygiene of their targets. One example is the breach of Ashley Madison and subsequent publication of the names and personal details of 32 million customers who used the company's website to facilitate extramarital affairs.[16]

- The security researchers who uncovered or analyzed the breach publicize it. For example, in May 2018, a security researcher published a report on a hacking campaign affecting over 300 websites, including those belonging to the San Diego Zoo and the government of Chihuahua, Mexico.[17]

- Reporting regulations compel an organization to disclose information about a breach. The loss of personal and financial information on nearly half the US population by Equifax—a large consumer credit ratings firm—is an example of this path to the public record.[18]

Media can't report on breaches or cyber incidents that are, in effect, secret, and many types of incidents, including theft of trade secrets, financial fraud, and extortion, often remain hidden.

Reader Demand

While the press plays an important role in civil society, there are some market factors that influence what it publishes. Specifically, it publishes content its readers want, and the trope "If it bleeds, it leads" translates in the digital world to covering breaches that are state sponsored (especially if the state's written language doesn't use Roman letters), ultra-sophisticated, never seen before, and the harbinger of imminent disaster, on either a national or a global scale. This story plays better than one about someone in the marketing department without any hacking skills who took R&D information because no one thought to protect it. Even if threats from competitors, partners, customers, suppliers, and employees are much more common and the financial impact usually greater, these stories are, well, boring and don't attract an audience.

Their roles, objectives, and incentives influence the voices of government, cybersecurity vendors, and the media. By understanding these influences, you'll be able to go beyond headlines to understand what really matters for you and your company. Now that we've laid out the cybersecurity landscape as it exists, in the rest of the book, we will show how you can lead your company to a new approach to cybersecurity that will effectively protect it, its shareholders, and the broader community of stakeholders.

PART TWO

The Principles

As a board member, you need to use your existing knowledge of business dynamics and operations to help your company execute an effective cybersecurity strategy, which includes understanding, managing, and reducing the risks to your business.

To accomplish this, you don't need to develop a completely new strategy. Nor will you need to fundamentally change the nature of your oversight. Instead, you will help your company expand its cybersecurity focus beyond technology and place the business, and risks to it, at the center of its decision making.

To assist you in this process, we developed four principles of digital stewardship with several considerations in mind. The first is they don't require any background in cybersecurity or computing technology. They're immediately actionable. Second, regardless of the amount of cybersecurity governance advice (this book included) you receive, you'll never be prepared for every situation or every decision you'll need to make. These principles provide guidance and can be used as rules of thumb when you encounter new circumstances.

You can also use these principles as a litmus test for how your company is managing its cyber-risk-related activities. Does the company follow the principles or not? In addition, you can then use them to guide your organization and the execution of its own cybersecurity oversight. These principles are further informed by understanding that your responsibilities are different from those of others inside your company—especially those for whom cybersecurity is a primary responsibility. The principles address dynamics and situations that are often outside the control or influence of cybersecurity specialists, yet are essential for their success.

4

If You Don't Understand It, They Didn't Explain It

Cybersecurity management and staff within a company are responsible for providing their board of directors with materials and briefings that nonspecialists can understand.

Current Situation

Cybersecurity briefings can cause frustration on both sides of a boardroom table. Some directors have noted to us that they're happy they are devoting more time to cybersecurity in full board and committee meetings, but they're often frustrated that the briefings and materials they receive from the company's cybersecurity team are not relevant or useful. Presentations are often repetitive, as if the team is struggling to find material to fill the time. Chief information security officers, on the other hand, grow frustrated with board members' apparent lack of interest in understanding what to them are elementary but important technical concepts.

Given differences in education, experience, and professional responsibilities, both reactions are understandable.

Consequences

Without relevant and understandable information, you can't assess your company's activities, current approach, resilience, or capacity to respond to attacks. Confusing presentations also impair your ability to assess whether current or future investments are suitable and effective. Furthermore, if you're not fully informed, you'll find yourself facing a Hobson's choice. You'll need to either approve funding without a clear idea of how your investment will reduce risks and protect your business, or disapprove funding and risk recriminations and second-guessing should a cyber incident occur later.

Because of this information asymmetry, a common practice is to delegate oversight to cybersecurity or IT teams. When this happens, you're placing your complete faith in the capabilities and judgment of individuals without understanding their tasks and objectives. If you don't understand what the cybersecurity technologists are doing, then you can't question or oversee their actions and spending.

Path Forward

You need to insist that cybersecurity professionals express their findings and recommendations in an understandable and relatable way. They can accomplish this by providing information in the context of your company and its business activities. Knowing the maturity of a cyber-security control isn't meaningful unless you understand its relevance to the risk protection of your business. The following chapter, "It Is the Business at Risk," offers an approach for accomplishing this by establishing the relationship among business risks, the types of cyberattacks that can cause these business risks, and the controls to prevent or mitigate cyberattacks.

Without this clear linkage between business risk and the cause of cyberattacks, cybersecurity briefings will be confusing—like listening to news coverage of cricket without knowing the ins and outs of the sport. Terms like "batsman" and "bowler" will be unfamiliar, let alone the mechanics of how a game or, rather, "match" is played.

5

It Is the Business at Risk

All discussions and actions relating to cybersecurity and cyber risks start and end with the business and the business risks to its operations and strategic direction, not with computers and their vulnerabilities.

Current Situation

The standards, products, and services available to cybersecurity teams don't make the job of addressing cyber risks any easier. In fact, they reinforce the message that cybersecurity is about protecting computers, not businesses. Globally recognized cybersecurity standards, such as the NIST cybersecurity framework and the ISO 27000 series, identify controls for protecting computers and the data that resides in them. These standards don't address how the controls can assist in protecting critical business functions from a cyberattack. As we mentioned earlier, the oversight was not on the part of the drafters of the standards, but rather an inherent limitation in the standards themselves, which are designed for use by a wide variety of organizations.

Cybersecurity products and services have similar limitations. For example, antivirus products protect against malicious software, firewalls protect against internet-based intrusions, and encryption can protect data that is lost or stolen. These solutions are useful for specific problems but, as such, can't address the larger picture of protecting a business. Commercial considerations further encourage vendors to focus on protecting computers and not businesses. The addressable market for a generic, computer-focused cybersecurity tool is much greater, and the development cost much lower, than an offering that addresses specific business risks for individual companies.

Consequences

External factors do not encourage specialists to look beyond the technical protection of computer systems. In addition, focusing on protecting computers because of the value in many of these activities, such as installing software security updates, has a seductive allure. The problem is that it's easy to spend all your time and money on computer-centric activities and never get around to addressing the fundamental issue, which is protecting your company.

When your cybersecurity controls are not informed by an understanding of how your business operates, there are two outcomes. First, the controls may interfere with conducting business, as was the case with the autoworkers whose external partners could no longer access valuable information because it was "safely" moved to the company's intranet. "Security gets in the way of doing business" is a common bromide because of just this type of situation. We prefer the phrasing "poorly designed cybersecurity gets in the way of doing business." Understanding how a business operates is the way to get the design right.

Another outcome of a computer-based focus is incomplete protection of your business. If a cybersecurity team doesn't know the details of how a business activity is conducted, it won't be able to ensure the business is properly protected.

Path Forward

Without external incentives and market forces to promote inclusion of business activities and operations in developing cybersecurity protections, your company needs an alternative incentive. Given your governance and oversight responsibilities, you're ideally situated to provide this incentive.

The aide-mémoire "Manage Cyber Risks" includes questions you can ask to ensure your company adopts this business focus. It all starts by recognizing the necessity of expanding the focus of cyber-risk-reduction activities beyond protecting computers.

Execution is the second step, and this important follow-through requires cooperation and shared responsibilities. It is not sufficient for corporate leaders to direct cybersecurity (or IT) management to make the company secure. Corporate leaders need to hold business managers accountable for providing enough information about their operations to the cybersecurity group so that cyber defenses support, instead of interfere with, business operations.

Thomas's previous book, *Digital Defense*, introduced the concept that "all measures to secure a company's information and systems that are not based on an understanding of what a company does are inherently incomplete because they can only protect against generic attacks on a company's computers."[1] How do you make sure your company isn't falling into this common trap? Ask yourself two questions:

> For each information asset and automated business process your company has, what security technologies protect it?

> For each security technology, which information assets and automated business processes does this protect?

If you can't answer the first question, then you have no reason to believe your company is protected. If you can't answer the second question, then you have no reason to believe that your company is spending its information security budget wisely."[2]

6

Make Cybersecurity Mainstream

In both corporate organization and activities, take cybersecurity from siloed functions and incorporate it into mainstream operations.

Current Situation

In most companies, people broadly agree that cybersecurity is a high priority. They share a similarly broad perception, though, that the cybersecurity or IT department is responsible for protecting the company from cyberattacks. The common metrics that measure cybersecurity spending as a percentage of overall IT budget provide evidence. Employees share a related perception that their cybersecurity responsibilities end with choosing strong passwords and then not writing them down. They don't see cybersecurity as part of their job description. Backing up this view is the idea that cybersecurity is so complicated that laypeople are simply incapable of making any meaningful contribution to their company's defenses. Cybersecurity, they think, is a matter best left to the experts.

Consequences

Isolating the cybersecurity or IT security functions within a company results in the same negative consequences as focusing on protecting computers instead of the business activities they support and automate. The Asian automobile company we referenced in chapter 2 provides a case in point. The decision of the IT department to put the R&D network inside the corporate intranet, as well the employees' creation of fake employee accounts for contractors to access the intranet, were made without any communications between the R&D and IT security departments because there were no organizational or operational connections between the two groups.

The initial breach that resulted in the billion-dollar loss was not the work of a nation-state or an organized crime group or even a lone-wolf criminal. It was the work of someone in the marketing department who had no cyber hacking skills at all. What the marketing staffer did have was authorized access to the R&D information, and she used that access to download the files and take them out of the company. At the time, many products could have prevented the theft and corresponding financial loss. However, just as with the R&D department, there was no organizational cybersecurity connection. Further, members of the IT security group, located in California, and the marketing department, located in Asia, quite literally didn't speak the same language.

Organizational and operational isolation of cybersecurity capabilities within a company has a profoundly negative impact on cyber protections. Business groups often assume the cybersecurity group is already addressing the cybersecurity risks arising from their activities, so it's not their concern. This in turn means missed opportunities for the cybersecurity group to engage with the business groups.

Path Forward

A dedicated cybersecurity group is clearly of value. Any company with a board of directors would be remiss not to have one. However, unless this specialized group of cyber experts understands the business and its goals, and the organization uses that knowledge throughout, its actions will be like the proverbial tree that falls silently in a forest because no one hears it.

There are several approaches to ensuring that the cybersecurity expertise in your company has an impact, and makes a noise, one of which is organizational:

- Place the cybersecurity group within a line function, particularly one with significant cyber risks, as opposed to a staff function, such as IT.

- Embed cybersecurity staff within business units.

- Develop in-house cybersecurity expertise within the business units at greatest risk.

Moving members of the cybersecurity team inside some business units might not be feasible in the near term. In any event, formal processes ensuring that cybersecurity review and input are provided—and acted upon—at critical junctures within business activities are a powerful tool. These reviews, described in chapter 9, should center on detection of changes that can introduce new cyber risks. Such potentially risky changes include:

- The development of a new product or service

- Reorganizations resulting from a merger, acquisition, or establishment of a joint venture

- Technological upgrades, such as moving a business function to the cloud

7

Engage Motivation

Understand and align the interests and motivations of staff and departments to incentivize behavior that leads to accomplishing cybersecurity goals.

Current Situation

Motivating employees, often through financial incentives, is a common practice. But motivation is seldom considered in the context of cybersecurity. The effectiveness of cybersecurity activities is often undercut because companies don't reward positive behavior. Worse, by offering well-intentioned incentives such as bonuses for meeting delivery deadlines, companies can actually discourage good cybersecurity work. If companies incentivize employees to meet aggressive deadlines, they're sure to reduce or curtail cybersecurity. Steven Kerr, former head of learning and leadership development at General Electric and Goldman Sachs, wrote more broadly about this dynamic in his article "On the Folly of Rewarding A, While Hoping for B."[1] This dynamic plays out through entire companies, including both staff with dedicated cybersecurity responsibilities and employees for whom cybersecurity tasks are just a part of their overall jobs.

Knowing what behavior to incentivize is another challenge. Executives have extensive experience in motivating employee performance when the deliverables are clear and concrete, such as meeting a sales quota. Incentivizing cybersecurity results, such as successful defense against cyberattacks, is more complicated because it is difficult to account for all the activities and decisions that could have taken place much earlier, on someone else's watch, that shaped the outcome. Further, should you reward employees for sound cybersecurity practices or is this just part of their job? Doctors, for example, don't receive bonuses for not killing patients, and pilots are not paid extra for landing a plane safely.

Consequences

A US-headquartered, global financial services firm provides an example of how the personal motivations and interests of individual IT staff rendered the firm's firewalls largely ineffective. Firewalls are designed to block connections from the internet that a hacker could use to attack computers within the corporate network, while at the same time permitting legitimate connections to business applications, such as customer self-service. IT staff people accomplish this by writing firewall rules that state what communications are or are not permitted. Since business applications come and go over time, IT staff need to review and update the rules. When we asked the IT staff at the financial services firm how frequently they reviewed and updated firewall rules, they said, "Never." Further into the conversation, the reason became clear. If the company experienced a cyberattack, in part because of faulty firewall rules, it would not blame the IT staff personally, especially if it suspected a nation-state was behind the attack.

If, however, the staff updated the firewall rules and accidentally blocked access to a business application, they would suffer immediate consequences and would need to remedy the situation as quickly as possible.

An Asia-based multinational insurance company illustrates how the motivation to accomplish a corporate strategy can undercut cybersecurity. The company was on a spending spree to achieve targets for an aggressive acquisition-driven growth strategy. Independently, the board had commissioned an audit of cyber risks. Interestingly, the scope of the audit was limited to the core business and excluded the business development function and the M&A deal flow. Because the pressure to grow was so high, management did not want to introduce any risk of slowing down the deal pipeline, even if it meant introducing new cyber risks into the core business or overpaying for deals that were impaired due to preexisting cybersecurity problems.

Path Forward

You should assume employees and managers will put their own immediate and personal interests above your company's cybersecurity needs. Both the IT staff who refused to update their firewalls and the automobile engineers who designed an unsafe work-around to help outside contractors access their company's intranet illustrate this point. To blame these individuals for acting in their best interests isn't useful and misses the point that companies are largely responsible for determining what their employees' best interests are.

Understanding employees' day-to-day motivations is the key to more effective cybersecurity. If your company makes cybersecurity decisions that are informed by understanding employee motivation, it will be far better protected from cyber threats than would result from installing the latest version of a cybersecurity product.

PART THREE

The Responsibilities

The responsibilities we describe in the following three chapters are the foundation of your digital stewardship. In fulfilling your responsibilities, you show your company the fundamental activities it must undertake, the dynamics it should consider, and the results it must deliver. Only you can provide this leadership, the essence of cybersecurity leadership.

As the foundation, these responsibilities address the most critical cybersecurity objectives your company must achieve:

- Identification of cyber risks within the context of business priorities and value

- Seamless integration of cybersecurity activities within the fabric of business activities

- Leadership and effective response in the event of a cyber crisis

Digital stewardship extends to include responsibilities such as engaging stakeholders, navigating regulations, and cultivating talent. All these rely on the foundation you are building.

8

Manage Cyber Risks

Your company's primary cybersecurity responsibility is to manage the cyber risks it faces. Your corresponding governance duty is to ensure that your company identifies, understands, manages, and monitors cyber risks according to a clear set of business priorities.

To meet your obligation, you need to address a number of overlapping questions, including:

- What cyber risks do we face?

- How could a cyberattack impact our business?

- Is our executive team engaged in prioritizing cybersecurity risks?

- Are we investing in the right areas to defend ourselves from cyberattacks?

- Are our cyber defenses effective?

The following practical steps will help you answer these questions and more. To aid this process, we recommend that you take a fresh look at three elements of cyber risk management:

1. *The meaning of cyber risk.* Think of cyber risks in the context of the business risks that cyberattacks can cause.

2. *The role of cybersecurity controls.* View cybersecurity controls from the perspective of the business activities they protect, not just the technical attacks they prevent.

3. *Determinants of effectiveness.* Look beyond the technical capabilities of cybersecurity products and services to the nontechnical factors that determine success.

Identify Cyber Risks

To meet your oversight responsibilities for cyber risk identification, you must ensure that your company:

- Identifies cyber risks in the context of your company's critical business activities and the risks to them

- Engages executive management in the process of cyber risk identification and business impact assessment

Connecting Cyber Risks to Business Risks

Richard Lancaster, the CEO of CLP, Asia's third largest electricity provider, describes his company's view of cyber risks: "Initially, we viewed cyber risks primarily as an IT issue. Over time, we realized that our generation and transmission systems were also at risk. Now we recognize cyber risk is really business risk, and my job as

CEO is to manage business risk."[1] Executives and experts agree with Lancaster's views. The challenge is to connect the two in a way that supports board and executive engagement and provides clear guidance on cyber risk mitigation. The key is to decide where to start the connection process.

The most common approach is to start with some technical method of cyberattack, such as malicious software or cracking passwords, and to then imagine the negative business outcomes that could result. Current market forces promote this approach. Vendors sell products, for example, to detect malicious software and increase the security of the log-in process, and standards describe general approaches for dealing with these types of threat. The challenge is that there is no basis for connecting a generic cyber risk with a business risk relevant to your company. Knowing that malicious software is a threat provides no actionable guidance in identifying the specific business risks it could cause.

A more practical approach starts with identifying your company's most critical business activities and the risks they face. From this starting point, your company's cybersecurity group can identify how a cyberattack could cause the business risks to materialize. For example, imagine you're on the board of a company that makes industrial products. You already understand the importance of your company's production lines and the risks posed by tropical storms, power outages, or equipment failure. Now, ask the question: How could a cyberattack disrupt your company's production lines?

Think of robots. Among the benefits of automation is the relative ease with which an assembly line can be reconfigured to manufacture a different product simply by uploading a new program into the computers controlling the robots. This very flexibility makes your company vulnerable to a cyberattack. To disrupt your production line, a cyber adversary could change the computer programs that control the robots, which could cause the robots to operate incorrectly or stop working altogether. This approach of starting first with the business activity gives your cybersecurity team clear direction on what it needs to do—protect the integrity of robotic software—to prevent a business risk from occurring.

This adjustment might seem like a minor change in the way you think about cyber risk, but the shift in mindset is profound. By starting with the business activity of manufacturing, general risks to this activity, and how computerized systems support it, you, other board members, and your company as a whole can clearly see the connection between business risk and cyber risk, and then use this insight to develop cyber defenses.

Developing Cyber Threat Narratives

After you've addressed cyber risks in the context of the associated risks to business activities, you need to establish a common basis of information for discussions and decisions. Prioritizing and fixing cyber risks is a social process, not just a technical task. Everyone, from executives, senior managers, and cybersecurity specialists to IT teams, will have their own perspectives and opinions. But you need to establish consensus in order to move forward with a unified sense of purpose and direction.

Telling a story is a common approach to collecting and organizing information to share across a wide audience. We developed cyber threat narratives that include four elements (see table 8-1).

To develop the cyber threat narratives, different parties cooperate in compiling and analyzing the information. In addition to executives and their management teams, they include:

- *Operations:* Personnel involved in day-to-day business activities, such as automobile designers, radiology billing clerks, and marketing staff

TABLE 8-1

Four elements of cyber threat narratives

Element	Purpose
Critical business activity and risks	Identification of a critical business activity and the risks it faces
Supporting systems	Identification of the computer systems on which a business activity relies
Cyberattacks and consequences	Cyberattacks that can cause critical business activity risks to materialize and their impact
Cyber adversaries	Identification and characterization of likely attackers

- *Systems:* People responsible for the administration of the computing systems supporting business activities

- *Cybersecurity:* Experts in the technical aspects of cyberattack and defense

- *Specialists:* Staff with different expertise, such as legal, public relations, human resources, and physical security

Let's look at each element within a cyber threat narrative.

Critical Business Activity and Risks

The first element of a narrative is the identification and description of a critical business activity, the benefits it provides, and the risks it faces. For example, for the chemical company we've talked about, that could be the manufacture of aromatic and polyester resins.

The critical nature of a business activity varies among companies and industries. For example, customer support is a low-risk activity for many companies. But, if you run a casino, customer support is critical. Casinos in the former Portuguese colony of Macau, for example, rely on a small segment of VIP customers, or "whales" as they are commonly referred to, for more than 54 percent of combined gross gaming revenue.[2] Attracting and retaining these players requires significant investments, such as complementary use of private jets and expansive suites with room service from Michelin-starred restaurants. For the casinos, risks to customer relationship management threaten their bottom line.

Once a business activity is identified as critical, the next step is sizing up inherent risks. There are two types of risk you should focus on. Of primary concern are risks that prevent your company from reaping the benefits of a business activity. For example, in the case of the chemical company, a disruption to its manufacturing operations (risk) would prevent it from making resins (consequence), which would lower its revenue (benefit).

There are also collateral risks that can harm your company, customers, or other stakeholders. In the case of a chemical manufacturing company, a release of poisonous chemicals into the environment is one example. The most publicized collateral risk is the loss of confidential customer information such as passwords and credit card information.

Sometimes, both types of risk can converge. When casinos cultivate VIPs, they provide more than luxurious perks; they also collect data such as time spent playing, average stake per hand, average number of hands per hour, and skill level. This information helps casinos optimize a high roller's gambling experience, as well as their own profits. A VIP's financial information is also valuable, but this information extends far beyond credit card details. Knowledge of offshore bank accounts and global real estate holdings increases a casino's comfort in extending credit, and collecting on it. The competition to attract VIP players is fierce, as a single individual can contribute millions or more to the bottom line. In the hands of a competitor, this data could be used to identify and lure away a casino's most profitable customers. In the hands of tax authorities or criminals, this data could pose a material threat to a VIP's overall financial circumstances.

When going through this exercise, don't assume every potential risk to a business activity should be a concern. In 2006, we met with an independent nonexecutive director for a *Fortune* 500 hard-drive manufacturer at its headquarters in Silicon Valley. The walls of the boardroom were lined with framed, gold-plated copies of patents, testaments to the company's history of innovation. Given this display, you would think that theft of intellectual property was a significant risk. But, as it turned out, intellectual property wasn't much of a concern at all. The company had cross-licensed patents with all major competitors and moved manufacturing to Malaysia, which, along with its neighbors Singapore and Thailand, accounted for 80 percent of total global production.[3] The company's advantage, therefore, came from producing large volumes of hard drives at competitively low unit costs, all while maintaining high product quality and reliability. Its competitive advantage was based on innovations such as shop floor design, supply chain management, quality assurance, and personnel management.

What poses a significant risk for one company may not for another. Although the disruption of resin production would be harmful to the chemical supply company, a similar disruption to another chemical manufacturer may not be. Maybe the chemical it uses is not in high demand, or its contribution to the bottom line is negligible, or alternative sources are readily and easily available.

Your oversight responsibility for this step is to gain assurance that:

☐ Your company has identified its most critical business activities, the benefits they provide, and the most significant business risks they face

The aide-mémoire for this step is Risk Inquiry 1 in chapter 11.

New, Cyber-Induced Business Risks

The power of cyberattacks can introduce new business risks that were previously of much less concern. The sensitivity of medical information is one example. The black-market demand for patient information is increasing dramatically, with complete medical records selling for more than $1,000.[4] Hospitals and their regulators have noticed this trend. In 2017, the Advocate Health Care hospital network paid a $5.5 million fine to the US Health & Human Services Department for three separate 2013 breaches that compromised the data of 4 million people. While clearly the loss of patient data is a risk that hospitals need to address, a more chilling risk arises not from someone stealing patient information, but from changing it.

Imagine a competitive situation between two hospital networks in which market supremacy yields significant financial returns. How could you lure patients away from a competing hospital to your doors? By hacking into your competitor's computer systems and changing patient medications, dosages, diagnoses, and surgical instructions. The wrong medication or too much of the right one can sicken or kill a patient. Changing "left" to "right" in a patient's medical record before kidney removal surgery is a death sentence for the patient and may as well be one for the hospital. And not because of malpractice lawsuits. The net result of these types of cyberattacks will erode people's trust in the hospital. Who would go to a hospital where they are just as likely to be killed as cured?

The military and intelligence communities have long been concerned with the integrity of information; formal cybersecurity work on the topic was published in 1975.[5] With the ever-increasing automation of business activities, commercial ventures should also be concerned about integrity.

Supporting Systems

The target for a cyberattack is one or more of the computer systems that support a business activity. Therefore, to mount a cyber defense, your company needs to identify these computer systems and the services and functionality they provide.

Operations personnel should kick-start the discovery process because they are familiar with the computer systems and applications they use, and the consequences if the systems were to malfunction or cease to function. Systems staff, who maintain the computer systems and know the full scope of their role, including functions not visible to operations staff, should aid in the process, too. Generally, IT staff people fill this systems role for general-purpose computers, and engineers fill the role in industrial control systems environments.

Given the complexity of computer systems and networks, all the computer systems supporting a critical business activity need to be inventoried. The inventory must include the physical locations of the systems so that cyber incident response staff know where they need to go to fix things in the event of a cyberattack.

Your oversight responsibility for this step is to gain assurance that:

☐ Your company has up-to-date inventories of the computer systems its critical business activities rely on

The aide-mémoire for this step is Risk Inquiry 2 in chapter 11.

Cyberattacks and Consequences

CYBERATTACKS

The next element of a cyber threat narrative identifies and characterizes the different types of cyberattacks that could cause a business risk. This entails examining the approaches and requirements for a successful attack.

At its most basic level, a cyberattack employs a variety of techniques, known as "threat vectors," to exploit vulnerabilities in computer systems. As the first line of inquiry, cybersecurity staff people need to identify and correlate cyberattack techniques with inherent vulnerabilities in the supporting computer systems. For example, in the WannaCry incident, the cyberattack technique consisted of malicious software exploiting security programming mistakes in Microsoft applications. The inherent vulnerability was running applications that had security-relevant programming mistakes.

Attacks are not always sophisticated or technically complex. For example, one vulnerability common to all computers is an administrator's almost complete control over the information and applications on it. This power is necessary for proper operation and maintenance, but an administrator can abuse it. In this case, the attack technique is nothing more than an administrator deciding to misuse her power.

In the manufacturing disruption example, an adversary could take two basic approaches to corrupt a robot's software instructions. One uses features within a robot to gain control over the process to upload instructions. Depending on the robot design, this may or may not require a password or special permission. Alternatively, the adversary could use malware that exploits a vulnerability in the robot's own underlying computer systems and bypass all restrictions on uploading instructions. In both cases, the adversary would need to connect to the robot using a network connection or plugging a USB or other device into it.

EXTENT OF IMPACT

Cyberattacks are not limited by geography. An attack can originate anywhere in the world and quickly spread across an entire enterprise through its corporate networks. For example, the pilfering of some 94 million credit cards from TJX, a multinational retailer with two thousand stores in North America and Europe, started in a suburban strip-mall parking lot in Miami, when a hacker gained access to the Wi-Fi networks of two of the company's Marshalls-branded discount clothing stores from his car.[6] This shows the sweeping pain a cyberattack can inflict. Not only was the entire Framingham, Massachusetts–based company hurt by what happened in Miami, but all of its brands, not just Marshalls, were affected. Customers at its larger, namesake TJ Maxx brand were also swept up by what happened.

The scale and volume of damage resulting from a cyberattack can be far more extensive than that associated with many other types of attack and criminal activity. In the case of intellectual property theft, the amount of trade secrets and other proprietary information that someone can transmit electronically out of a company vastly exceeds what they can carry out the door.

The trend of increasing digital control over critical infrastructure further expands the extent of impact. For example, coordinated cyberattacks on three Ukrainian electricity companies in December 2015 left the 230,000 residents of Ivano-Frankivsk without electricity for up to six hours.[7] Recent analysis of the hacking tool that caused this outage shows that it could be used on a much larger scale.[8] Perhaps the most pertinent reason cyberattacks result in consequences far exceeding other causes is because there is an adversary behind the attack.

ATTACK REQUIREMENTS

Not all cyberattacks are created equal. Nor are all equally easy to carry out. In order to know the types of cyberattacks you and your company should worry about, you first must ensure your company understands what an adversary needs to mount a successful cyberattack. The three types of cyberattack prerequisites are:

1. *Knowledge* covers what an adversary needs to know; it can range from programming malicious software to managing the systems used to operate hydroelectric dams.

2. *Tools and equipment* include not only hacking tools, but equipment such as laptops and radio transmitters.

3. *Position* is where an adversary is and can either be geographic (for example, a point on a map) or organizational (for example, an employee or contractor).

In the debit card fraud we examined at a Southeast Asian bank, the required knowledge included the format of Visa and Mastercard authorization codes and how to configure a credit card terminal. The tools included several of the terminals, along with a database of debit card account numbers. The attackers had to be in the local vicinity to coordinate with merchants who were complicit with the fraud but didn't necessarily need to work at the bank or get inside.

In addition to considering the feasibility of different types of cyberattacks, think about how an adversary could use easier, noncyber means to compromise a business activity. For example, an insurance company operating in Asia initially was concerned that its agents might write policies against which they would submit fraudulent claims by exploiting potential vulnerabilities in the mobile application. But, after realizing that it would be much simpler for an agent to use a friend or relative to accomplish the same goal, the company dropped its concern.

CONSEQUENCES

While your company's cybersecurity group has the primary responsibility for developing cyberattack descriptions, your operations and systems staff can help in understanding consequences. A series of "What if . . . ?" questions can form the basis for this collaboration. What would happen to the provision of care, for example, if a hospital's patient records were no longer accessible because of a ransomware attack? For England's National Health Service in the aftermath of WannaCry, the answer was the "cancellation of thousands of appointments and operations."[9]

Some consequences go beyond strict financial loss. The NotPetya cyberattack of 2017 interrupted operations and resulted in financial loss for numerous large companies worldwide, including AP Moller-Maersk with an estimated price tag of US$200 to $300 million and FedEx at US$400 million.[10] Pharmaceutical giant Merck estimated NotPetya's impact at US$670 million because of both direct costs and lost revenue.[11]

The consequences for Merck's customers could have been much worse. The NotPetya attack crippled Merck's manufacturing processes, including those for its cancer vaccine, which is recommended for children starting at age eleven or twelve.[12] Fortunately, Merck was able to borrow doses from the US Centers for Disease Control and Prevention's stockpile to fill the demand it couldn't meet. If Merck hadn't had access to the stockpiled doses, the consequences would have gone beyond a loss on the books to increased risk of cancer in young people.

Executive leadership and senior management are well positioned to identify risks to these activities and the consequences. Specialists from other departments, such as legal, finance, and compliance, can help further identify collateral risks. Meetings with executive leadership are critical, but they don't need to be time-consuming. Well-scripted interviews and discussions are efficient ways to collect and document executive input.

Your primary oversight responsibility for this element of a cyber threat narrative is to ensure your company has identified:

☐ The most significant types of cyberattacks that can cause critical business activity risks to materialize

☐ The ranges of possible impact to both your company and its stakeholders

The aide-mémoire for this step is Risk Inquiry 3 in chapter 11.

Cyber Adversaries

Cyberattacks are not natural disasters; they don't just happen. Someone is behind them. The question is, Who's out to get you? The answer could be countries, criminal organizations, competitors, disgruntled employees, terrorists, or advocacy groups. CLP's Lancaster observed, "The cyber threat landscape is changing. Critical infrastructure, especially electric power, is increasingly a target of cyberattack. The adversaries who concern us are well funded and organized criminals and nation states."

Identifying potential adversaries, as well as their motivations and capabilities, can help your company assess the likelihood of a cyberattack and determine the controls it will need to thwart it. As we described in chapter 2, advanced hacking tools are widely available to many potential cyber adversaries. This increases the importance of other capabilities such as financing, staffing, and logistics.

Think about what your company has that could be of value to someone else. For example, a competitor could be interested in your R&D and trade secrets, whereas a criminal organization would be more interested in stealing customer financial records to sell on the black market.

Even customers are potential cyber adversaries. AMSC (formerly known as American Superconductor Corp.) was a profitable company that developed software for controlling wind turbines in its headquarters in Devens, Massachusetts. In 2011, Sinovel, one of its largest customers, suddenly canceled payments on all delivered products and future contracts, worth over $800 million. An investigation revealed that Sinovel had bribed one of AMSC's European developers to steal the software so it wouldn't have to pay for it, and then proceeded to deploy the software to more than a thousand turbines in China. In July 2018, seven years after the theft, a US court awarded AMSC $59 million, some of which has been paid. However, this doesn't come close to approaching the loss of over a billion dollars in AMSC's shareholder equity and seven hundred jobs, which was over half of its global workforce.[13] As a result of this intellectual property theft, AMSC reported a loss of over $186 million in fiscal year 2010 and revenues have never returned it to profitability.[14]

Also consider a potential adversary's larger business and commercial situation. During our meeting with casino managers on the Coati Strip in Macau, they told us about the customer relationship management system they used to collect, analyze, and monetize the wealth of proprietary data they had on VIP clients. Data was constantly collected from multiple locations across Macau and transmitted via the local telecommunication network to a centralized operations center. When asked about these networks, the casino managers replied that the network connections were not encrypted. They had not identified the need. The next question we asked was, Who owns the telecommunications firm? It was as if all the air was sucked out of the room. The casino operators realized that the telecommunications firm, which had unlimited access to their most sensitive customer information as it traversed their network, was owned by a conglomerate that included their largest gaming competitor.

Sometimes a company's industry or the way in which it conducts business could motivate someone to mount an attack against it. For example, environmental groups might target companies with a bad record for polluting. Edward Snowden, a former NSA contractor, stole information from the NSA to expose surveillance programs that it publicly denied.[15] In another case, the group Anonymous mounted cyberattacks against five oil companies—Shell, BP, Exxon, Gazprom, and Rosneft. The group held these companies responsible for what it thought was harmful action in the Arctic.[16] Company activities, such as layoffs or plant closures, can also motivate employees to misuse their computer privileges as a means of retaliation.

For another perspective, look beyond your company to the broader commercial and political world in which it operates. For instance, if as suspected, Russia was behind the cyberattacks on power plants in Ivano-Frankivsk in 2015, the motivations for the attacks likely had nothing to do with the power companies themselves. The companies were probably targeted simply because they are located in the Ukraine, a country with which Russia has a hostile relationship.

Senior executives are well positioned to identify entities that may want to attack the company. But there will be surprises. The WannaCry attack had an impact on a wide variety of companies worldwide, and the only thing connecting the victims was the fact that they hadn't patched their systems. And there will always be random individuals with a personal agenda to pursue or reputation to enhance.

From an oversight perspective, your job is to ensure that your company:

☐ Identifies likely cyber adversaries, their capabilities, and motivations—and the characteristics that make your company a target

The aide-mémoire for this step is Risk Inquiry 4 in chapter 11.

When Hedge Funds Become Cyber Adversaries

In 2016, MedSec, a cybersecurity research firm specializing in the health-care industry, published a report on vulnerabilities in pacemakers and defibrillators made by St. Jude Medical, an multinational medical device manufacturer later acquired by Abbott Laboratories. Previously, MedSec had spent eighteen months examining medical devices from a wide variety of vendors, and in the words of MedSec CEO Justine Bone, "St. Jude stood out far and away as severely deficit when it comes to security protections."[17] Among the more noteworthy vulnerabilities MedSec found in St. Jude's pacemakers was the ability to change pacemaker settings, for example, stop pacing and drain the battery from fifty feet away. According to Bone, other security researchers had approached St. Jude with similar results in 2013, but St. Jude didn't act on the information.

Thinking that St. Jude similarly wouldn't act on its findings, MedSec adopted a different approach to draw attention to the vulnerabilities and prompt St. Jude to act. MedSec contacted Muddy Waters, an investment firm with a long history of shorting stocks. By shorting, Muddy Waters stood to profit if St. Jude's stock price dropped in value. MedSec allegedly coordinated the release of the security report with Muddy Waters' shorting of St. Jude stock, with the agreement that both companies would share the resulting profits. Public opinion quickly coalesced against MedSec and Muddy Waters, and St. Jude responded with vigorous denials and a defamation lawsuit.[18]

An investigation by the US Department of Homeland Security and the Food and Drug Administration (FDA) ensued

(Continued)

amid the controversy.[19] The FDA issued an alert of its own that 460,000 pacemakers were vulnerable and should have their software updated. However, unlike corporate computers that can be remotely updated en masse, updating these pacemakers was a major undertaking. The 460,000 people with implanted pacemakers needed to visit their doctors, who could perform the update. Unfortunately, in a small number of cases, some of the procedures could result in a "complete loss of device functionality."[20]

This case provides several interesting observations about cyber adversaries and cyberattacks. It was not a cyberattack that caused the damage. Evidence that a cyberattack could succeed damaged St. Jude's reputation and sparked a recall. Second, the damaging way the risk was disclosed, aiming to drive down the stock price and enrich short sellers, hurt all shareholders and not just St. Jude. The case also adds profit-minded hedge funds and cybersecurity research firms to the list of potential cyber adversaries—as if the list wasn't long enough already. Finally, St. Jude's perceived reluctance to remedy a potential cybersecurity shortcoming provided motivation for its cyber adversary.

The Expressive Power of Cyber Threat Narratives: Maroochy Shire

One cyber crisis illustrates how its salient features correspond to the elements of a cyber threat narrative. This incident further confirms how narratives are a convenient and easily understandable way to explain the technical details of cyberattack and defense. The first principle of digital stewardship—if you don't understand it, they didn't explain it—is achievable.

Maroochy Shire is a pastoral community and tourist destination located about a hundred kilometers north of Brisbane, Australia, on Queensland's Sunshine Coast, where the Pacific Ocean is warm all year and the perennial weather forecast is "beautiful today, perfect tomorrow." The area is one of outstanding natural beauty and ecological significance, with long white beaches, stunning lakes, and subtropical rainforests with gorges, creeks, and waterfalls. It is a habitat for koalas as well as rare species such as the glossy black cockatoo and ground parrot.

Within the shire, Maroochy Water Services served the community by managing all aspects of its water supply including water storage, treatment, and distribution, as well as the collection, treatment, and disposal of an average of 35 million liters of wastewater daily for businesses and residents.[21] This business activity is critical. Because of elevation variations in the shire, Maroochy Water Services' sewage systems required 142 pumping stations deployed at strategic points throughout its 880-kilometer network to pump wastewater to higher elevations so it could continue to flow by gravity on its path to the treatment facility.

Maroochy Water Services had a central operations system to manage the pumping stations. From this central point, operators could, among other actions, turn individual pumping stations on or off, as well as increase or decrease the pumping rates. Pumping stations could also be managed locally, and the on-site control equipment could instruct the central systems operations center to control the operation of other pumping stations.

In late January 2000, the central system that managed all the pumping stations started to behave strangely, such as losing communications and control over the pumps, as well as issuing false alarms.[22]

Weeks later, a vendor concluded that a person was attacking the control system computers, but it was too late. By the time the vendor had diagnosed the problem, raw sewage had backed out of pumping stations and flowed through the shire. Repeated releases encroached on neighborhoods, tidal canals, and even the PGA championship golf course of the formerly five-star Hyatt Regency Coolum Resort.[23] In the nearby township of Pacific Paradise, "up to a million liters of raw sewage ended up in a storm water drain."[24] In local parks and waterways, "marine life died, creek water turned black and residents endured a terrible stench."[25] All were the consequences of the cyberattacks.

The cyberattacks ended on the night of April 23 after the police found a suspect driving near a pumping station in the aptly named town of Deception Bay. In the suspect's car, the police found stolen pumping station control equipment, computers, network cables, and two-way radio equipment—the tools needed to mount the cyberattack. Over a period of nearly three months, the culprit's car served as his mobile control center as he carried out more than forty cyberattacks, causing the massive discharge of raw sewage into this once pristine environment.

The cyber adversary in this case was a former employee of the vendor that provided the pumping station control equipment. After a period of contentious employment with the vendor, he applied twice for employment with Maroochy Water Services but wasn't hired. As a result, he became disgruntled and resentful, and wanted to wreak revenge on both companies.[26] Since he knew how the control system worked, he was able to use radio equipment to communicate with individual pumping stations and cause the strange behavior that had been detected earlier.

The cyberattack used the very systems designed for the proper management of pumping stations to cause them to malfunction.

This attack involved two components: setting up a network connection to the control systems in individual pumping stations, and then manipulating the control systems both to cause local damage and to take over the central operations management system. In order to execute the cyberattack, the disgruntled ex-employee only needed to exploit two cybersecurity vulnerabilities. The first vulnerability was that a password wasn't required to log on to a pumping station's control equipment. The second was that the radio frequency used to communicate with the control equipment was easily available via company documentation. While the former employee needed to be within radio range, he did not need to physically break into a pumping station.

Although the attacker's insider status contributed to his success, the resources for pulling off similar attacks, once the sole province of employees and contractors, are now available to anyone with an internet connection. With a small bit of web searching, one can download communication protocols, product documentation, programming instructions, and software for the same equipment used in the pumping stations. In online forums, experts gladly answer questions and offer advice on the use of these kinds of equipment. Name-brand online retailers and auction sites have a healthy aftermarket for test kits and hardware, so attackers can plan and test their attacks from the comfort of their home or office anywhere in the world.

The scary thing is that the cyberattack could have been much worse. Technically, the attacker could have stopped all the pumping stations and flooded the community with raw sewage, which would have a created a bigger catastrophe. The scale of the impact was much worse, and much less expensive, than could have been achieved by a noncyber cause, such as blowing up a pumping station.

The Maroochy Water Systems case offers several lessons (see table 8-2). One is the importance of understanding how a cyberattack

TABLE 8-2

Four elements of cyber threat narrative at Maroochy Shire

Element	Maroochy Shire example
Critical business activity and risks	Activity: Wastewater treatment Risk: Pumping station malfunction
Supporting systems	Centralized operations management system Pumping station control equipment
Cyberattacks and consequences	Exploitation of insecure network communications and lack of user authentication on pumping station control equipment Massive release of raw sewage
Cyber adversary	Disgruntled former employee

can compromise the vulnerabilities in systems. The other is deciding on the right controls to thwart an attack. In this case, only two controls were needed: requiring passwords to log in to control equipment and encrypting radio communications. In contrast, since the perpetrator didn't use malicious software, common controls such as antivirus products or anti-phishing training would have offered no protection. Further, as you can see, the explanation of the technical mechanics of this cyberattack and the mitigating controls is easy to understand and is an example of the types of cyber risk descriptions your company should provide you.

Another lesson, as you go through the process of identifying cyber risks, is the importance of looking for cybersecurity design flaws. The lack of authentication for the control system and encryption of radio communication were technical flaws in the design of the control systems. The root causes of the debit card fraud we mentioned earlier were technical design flaws in the protocols for authorizing purchases and procedural design flaws in the timing of paying merchants and challenging charges. Only by identifying cyber risks in the context of a business activity can a company find these vulnerabilities.

Cyber Threat Narratives Focus Company Cybersecurity Activities

The use of cyber threat narratives as the framework for understanding your company's most significant cyber risks supports digital stewardship and effective corporate cyber risk management by:

Changing the conversation. The identification and prioritization of cyber risks shifts the conversation from a technical discussion to one firmly grounded in protecting your company's most important business activities and operations. Company leadership and management can participate in this process, and you and other board members can lead it.

Putting technical information in context. The ways in which your company collects, analyzes, and organizes technical information relating to cyberattack techniques, computer vulnerabilities, and computing infrastructure all contribute to developing the necessary knowledge for protecting the business activities leadership has prioritized.

Providing a practical approach. Your company needs to define information collection, analysis, and decision-making activities, and identify the types of staff who are best suited for each task. In all likelihood, your company already undertakes many of these tasks so it can easily develop cyber threat narratives by coordinating existing activities and using data already collected.

Fostering collaboration and consensus. The process of cyber threat narrative development provides a formal structure for contributions and collaboration across a wide range of staff from executive leadership and cybersecurity specialists to

(Continued)

those involved in the day-to-day conduct of business activities and those who manage the supporting computer systems. This promotes consensus around cyber risk priorities and the activities your company needs to undertake to address them.

Unifying cyber- and business-risk-related information. Cyber threat narratives contain a unified collection of information that establishes the relationship between cyberattacks and their potential risks to critical business activities. Groups and individuals within your company will use different slices of this information according to their roles and responsibilities. The thread that runs through all this information helps unify the entire company in identifying, prioritizing, and managing its most critical cyber risks.

Forming the foundation for all digital stewardship duties. The organization and presentation of cyber risks in the larger context of business risks builds the foundation for your company's cybersecurity-related activities. This includes the cyber risk management activities we address later in this chapter, as well as building corporate resiliency in the face of cyber-induced crises, which we address in the following chapter. Casting cyber risks in the context of business risks further informs organizational structure and corporate culture issues that directly influence your company's cyber risk management capability.

Facilitating board engagement and oversight. Your responsibilities are clear at every stage of narrative development. So are the assurances you need from the company you oversee in terms of the cyber-risk-related activities it has undertaken, topics it has addressed, people it has involved, and the documentation it has delivered.

Mitigate Attacks

From an oversight perspective, your responsibilities relating to cyber risk mitigation are to ensure that your company:

- Prioritizes cyber risks based on the impact their corresponding cyberattacks could inflict on your company's most critical business activities

- Selects controls based on the prioritized cyber risks they can effectively mitigate

- Examines control effectiveness

- Develops cyber risk remediation plans that directly connect controls to the business activities they protect

Prioritizing Cyberattacks

In practical terms, cyber risks are nothing more than cyberattacks that cause business risks to materialize. As such, the process of prioritizing cyber risks is really the process of prioritizing cyberattacks. Conveniently, all the information your company needs to undertake this prioritization can be found in the cyber threat narratives.

At the most fundamental level, the criteria for prioritizing cyberattacks are their capacity to cause damage to your company. The logical starting point, therefore, is the first element of cyber threat narratives, which describes your company's critical activities and the inherent business risks it faces. This recalls the second principle of digital stewardship—"It is the business at risk. All discussions and actions relating to cybersecurity and cyber risks start and end with the business and the risks to its operations and strategic direction, not with computers and their vulnerabilities."

After identifying these critical business activities and associated risks, the next step in the prioritization process is determining which risks are most susceptible to cyberattack. The remaining three cyber-threat-narrative elements inform this examination into impact and likelihood. Taking into account the supporting systems—the second element—the third element identifies the cyberattacks that could have an impact on a critical business activity, the requirements for a successful attack, and the degree and extent of the resulting impact. In particular, your company should look for cyberattacks that result in greater impact than possible from other causes and those that are simpler to execute. The final element to consider is the motivation and capabilities of likely adversaries, since cyberattacks don't happen on their own.

Your company's prioritization of cyberattacks, and therefore cyber risks, not only lays the groundwork for selecting controls to counter these attacks, but also informs cyber staffing and skills development. Through your oversight of this prioritization process, you are ensuring that the money your company spends on cybersecurity directly relates to reducing its most significant cyber and business risks.

Your oversight responsibility is to ensure that your company has prioritized cyberattacks on the basis of:

☐   Their capacity to cause risks to critical business activities

☐   The range of possible impacts

☐   The resources required for a successful attack

☐   The motivations and capabilities of likely cyber adversaries

The aide-mémoire for this step is Risk Inquiry 5 in chapter 11.

Selecting Controls

After prioritizing the cyberattacks to defend against, the next step is to choose the right tools for the job. The connections the company has established in the cyber threat narratives between cyberattack techniques and vulnerabilities in the supporting systems for business activities provide the basis for identifying the most suitable cyber risk controls. These controls logically fit between cyberattacks and supporting computer systems. One way of approaching control selection is to start with the prioritized cyberattacks and choose controls that mitigate the attacks. Cybersecurity standards, such as ISO/IEC 27002, "Information technology—Security techniques—Code of practice for information security controls," can be helpful resources because they describe the suitability of different controls to address common cybersecurity challenges.[27]

When a company selects controls to counter a cyberattack, it may find that a collection of controls is more effective than a single control. In the early days of corporate network perimeter defenses, firewalls were the technological solution of choice. Today, intrusion detection and protection systems and security log analysis, among other protection measures, complement firewalls. In the case of cyber defenses, the whole is definitely more than the sum of its parts, because the collection of controls can compensate for limitations in any individual one.

Collections of controls can extend beyond technology to physical and procedural controls. By looking at all three types of controls together, it is possible to address cyber risks more efficiently and cost-effectively than through technology alone. In the 1980s, we certified the cybersecurity functionality of computers inside nuclear missile silos. There was concern that some of the security requirements called for in Department of Defense standard 5200.28 could prevent the soldiers manning the missiles from fulfilling presidential orders. We took into account these operational concerns, the intended risk mitigation purposes of the cyber controls, and the protection the physical controls provided. We realized that the physical controls provided stronger assurances in the areas of authentication and accountability than security features in the computers deep inside the silos could accomplish. By incorporating physical protection into the mix, the selected controls provided higher security at lower cost than could be accomplished otherwise.

When selecting controls, companies need to look at how proposed controls will work in practice in the day-to-day running of a business. Without this business context, it is easy to make control choices that appear suitable on the surface, but either fail to protect the business activity or actually increase its risk exposure. A global financial institution with an annual cybersecurity budget measured in the hundreds of millions of dollars provides an example of what can happen if you ignore this business context. Employees at this company have valid business reasons to email sensitive information to outside parties ranging from large institutional partners to individual contractors. Interception of these emails as they traverse the internet is the cyber risk of primary concern.

To address this risk, the financial institution deployed its own encrypted email system to prevent interception and used a technology known as data loss prevention (DLP) to determine if an email contains sensitive information. DLP tools use a variety of techniques from pattern matching to sophisticated heuristics to identify sensitive information. Commonly, companies use these tools to prevent sensitive information from leaving. The financial institution used DLP to make sure any sensitive information that left the company was encrypted. The company only used the DLP system to check the contents of unencrypted emails, not encrypted emails. This meant that once an encrypted email connection was set up with a third party, an employee could send it any and all of the company's sensitive information, not just the sensitive information needed to conduct business. By not fully considering how the company conducted business communications, the cybersecurity department ironically built the very tools an insider could use to securely and covertly send out all the company's "crown jewels."

From an oversight perspective, your job is to ensure your company:

☐   Selects cyber controls on the basis on their suitability to mitigate the prioritized cyberattacks

The aide-mémoire for this step is Risk Inquiry 6 in chapter 11.

Examining Control Effectiveness

Once your company has identified the controls for mitigating the most significant types of cyberattacks, it should then examine if the controls will be effective. Because the company has not yet installed the controls, it can't test their functionality. However, considering the human element in two aspects of control use is a good indicator of future effectiveness: (1) the cybersecurity staff's management of controls, and (2) people's behavior when they confront controls.

Control Management

Dynamics that extend beyond a control's advertised features can impede its proper management and thus reduce its effectiveness. In chapter 7, we described how the dynamics at a financial services company discouraged IT staff from testing and properly configuring the company's firewalls because rigor in performing these tasks could result in criticism and increased work pressure for them individually.

Another factor impacting effectiveness is the increasing sophistication of technical controls and the resulting complexity in configuring, managing, and using them. For example, protecting a company's intranet and all the systems and information that support the conduct of its business uses a variety of controls. Those controls vary from firewalls and intrusion detection and prevention systems to the monitoring of network communications, both incoming and outgoing. Each of the devices involved in this intranet perimeter protection, as well as computers within a corporate intranet, capture and log events relevant to the performance of its individual piece of the protection pie. The individual logs record activities such as a failed password change or the disabling of antivirus software.

Examined individually, the logs provide limited value in detecting an internet-based attack. Combined and analyzed together, however, they are a powerful tool for detecting and responding to an attack. The market has responded with a variety of log collection and analysis tools. Their capacity to collate and analyze thousands or millions of individual log entries also becomes a drawback because of the challenges of knowing which log events to focus on and under what circumstances should people be alerted to investigate. To address this issue, vendors provide standard templates to address specific cybersecurity concerns, such as compliance with payment card cybersecurity standards.[28] The templates have the same inherent weakness of standards in general. They cannot know the specifics of an individual company's operations and so cannot provide an intelligent means of winnowing less relevant log records. The result is that cybersecurity staff find it challenging to use the log analysis tools to reduce cyber risks.

Cyber threat narratives address this issue by identifying the techniques associated with the cyberattacks that pose the greatest threat to the computer systems supporting a company's most critical business activities. Without this focus and direction, cybersecurity staff often find themselves in a similar position as the radio astronomers in the SETI program, futilely straining to hear alien signals in a universe of static.

Before its breach in 2013, Target, a large US-based retailer, had made significant investments in prominent vendors' sophisticated detection and logging capabilities. Thanks to this investment, the company received multiple warnings that its systems had been compromised before the breach, but didn't act on the warnings.[29] By its own admission, Target was constantly inundated with a "vast number of technical events that take place and are logged."[30] If Target had instead focused its substantial investments in log analysis and efforts on listening for signs of the most relevant cyberattack techniques, it might not have lost the subsequent alerts in the shuffle. It might have avoided the breach, which ultimately exposed the personal information of some 70 million customers.

Human Behavior

The log analysis tools we just discussed are an example of a cyber risk control that is transparent to all employees, except for the cybersecurity staff. Many other controls are not only broadly visible to employees, but directly affect them. The ways in which employees behave when presented with the controls can either negate the controls' protection value or introduce new cyber risks. In chapter 2, we discussed how the well-intentioned control of embedding the automobile design network within the company's intranet prompted the designers to create employee computer accounts for external partners, thus weakening the cybersecurity protection of the whole company. The automobile designers took action to deliberately undermine a control because it interfered with their ability to get their job done.

Failing to consider fully predictable human behavior can render a control ineffective and increase the risk or damage the control was intended to mitigate. The quotidian task of hand washing aptly illustrates this point. Thanks to opposable thumbs, our hands are quite handy at manipulating all sorts of things covered with bacteria and viruses. The naturally produced oils on the surface of our hands capture the germs and serve as the primary pathway for the pathogens to get inside us. In some cases, they can make us sick.

Handwashing with soap has long proved to be an effective control for this attack of germs and our body's vulnerability to getting sick. Soap chemically breaks down pathogen-containing oil on the hands and allows water to rinse the pathogens down the drain. Soap's five-thousand-year history as the preeminent hand-cleaning control was called into question in 1972, when antibiotics were added to soap.[31] Ostensibly, washing hands with antibacterial soap seems like a good thing, but since people tend to quickly wash their hands, antibiotics prove useless because they need to remain on the skin for two full minutes. Most of us are not this patient when washing our hands, and numerous scientific studies have confirmed the obvious, with one study pegging average hand-washing time at six seconds.[32] Not only are antibacterial soaps ineffective in practice, they have a negative impact on the environment by interfering with photosynthesis and have the potential to create antibiotic-resistant bacteria.

We can find a similar situation with cybersecurity policies surrounding passwords, perhaps the most visible and intrusive of all cybersecurity controls. Many companies require employees to change their passwords on a regular, sometimes monthly or quarterly, basis. Forcing this change is a control that addresses the risk that a hacker may have already uncovered current passwords by using personal information, lists of common passwords, and even complete dictionaries in automated searches. The rationale is that by regularly changing passwords, a hacker would have to start all over again each time an employee changes a password. All of this makes sense until one considers the limited ability people have to remember passwords.

We examined this situation at an Asia-headquartered financial services conglomerate. The password policy required users to change their password each month. They could not reuse previous passwords. Unsurprisingly, when we analyzed a sample of passwords, we discovered that the staff came up with creative ways to cope with the burden this policy imposed. One employee, for example, used this series:

- Password201801 (for January)

- Password201802 (for February)

- Password201803 (for March)

- And so on

While the passwords were easy for the employee to remember, they were equally easy for a hacker to predict. This practice undermines security, as frustrated users tend to create weak passwords in response.[33]

In addition to failing to take human behavior into account, password policies also don't consider available cyber controls. Thanks to password managers, first available in the mid-1990s, it is now easy to create long, unique, and random passwords for every website, application, and service you use without having to remember any of them. All you need to remember is the password for the password manager. For example, even with the computing resources necessary to make 100 trillion password guesses per second, it would still take over 600 billion, trillion, trillion centuries to crack a random thirty-character password, well beyond the remaining life of the universe. With a password this strong, you have no reason to ever change it unless you strongly suspect that it has been compromised as part of a cyberattack on the computer where you use the password. Should this happen, though, creating another thirty-character password is just a click away.

Your oversight responsibility is to ensure that your company:

☐ Has identified and is taking measures to overcome nontechnical impediments, such as human behavior, to the proper management of controls and the effectiveness of controls in practice

The aide-mémoire for this step is Risk Inquiry 7 in chapter 11.

Developing a Remediation Plan

The next step, after prioritizing cyber risks, selecting controls, and examining control effectiveness, is to develop a cyber risk remediation plan. Beyond customary details, such as schedules for deploying controls, the plan should answer a couple of questions starting with, Why is your company undertaking these cybersecurity activities? The answer draws on correlations among critical business activities, vulnerabilities in their supporting systems, the cyberattacks that could exploit the vulnerabilities, and the resulting impact on the business activities themselves. Your company can find this information in the cyber threat narratives.

In addition to providing a business-based rationale for cybersecurity priorities, a cyber risk remediation plan should answer the questions, When is enough enough? When has your company reduced its cyber risks to an acceptable level? While cyber risks need to be mitigated, and some investments may be substantial, cybersecurity budgets should never have a blank check.

Because the process of identifying and prioritizing cyber risks is closely tied to business risk, your company is well positioned to answer this question by analyzing the relationship between a cyberattack's capacity to disrupt or harm critical business activities and the strength of controls and related ongoing cybersecurity actions to reduce this capacity to an acceptable level. The analysis relies on cybersecurity input on control performance and executive input on acceptable business risk.

The outcome is that your company's cyber risk remediation plan becomes a statement of the activities and investments it needs to reduce its cyber risks to an acceptable level. Once the company deploys the controls, develops related capabilities, and puts ongoing processes in place, it is giving the business activities the level of cyber protection they need.

From an oversight perspective, your job is to ensure your company:

☐ Provides a cyber risk remediation plan that demonstrates how and when the deployment of selected controls, and associated activities, reduces your company's most critical cyber risks to an acceptable level

The aide-mémoire for this step is Risk Inquiry 8 in chapter 11.

9

Fortify the Company

After leading your company to approach cyber risks in the context of well-understood business risks, you now need to ensure that it is prepared to address cyber risks on an ongoing basis. This requires a well-thought-out organizational structure and processes supported by a culture that promotes openness and communication.

The first thing your company needs to know is where to look for new cyber risks. The good news is that it doesn't have to look far. Some new cyber risks have external origins, such as vulnerable commercial software. But nearly all the new cyber risks your company will face owe their origin to business-motivated changes that originate within your company. In order to capture these new risks, your company needs to have well-defined checkpoints within its change management processes for evaluating cyber risk and follow through on developing a cyber risk mitigation plan.

Your company should brief you regularly on its current cyber risk posture, as it relates to specific business activities. This chapter introduces a two-step process for determining your company's current posture, based on testing control performance and the degree of progress on the cyber risk mitigation plan.

In addition to processes for identifying and tracking new cyber risks, the placement of the cybersecurity group within your company plays a significant role in reducing your company's cyber risks. Part of your oversight responsibilities is to ensure that your company takes organizational alignment of mission and interests into account when finding a home for cybersecurity.

At the end of the chapter, we examine how commonly accepted norms of corporate behavior have the unintended consequence of keeping you, the rest of the board, and senior executives in the dark about what is really going on with cybersecurity inside your company.

Develop Institutional Cyber Risk Foresight

To meet your oversight responsibilities related to ongoing cyber risk management, you must ensure that the companies you oversee:

- Know where to look and what to look for to identify changes that can introduce new cyber risks

- Develop processes with well-defined checkpoints and assigned responsibilities to capture new cyber risks and create mitigation plans on an ongoing basis

Anticipating Cyber Risks

Attempts at earthquake prediction date back to at least the fourth century BC, when Aristotle reasoned in *Meteorologica* that earthquakes could be forecast by observing "an eclipse of the moon" or a "little, light, long-drawn cloud."[1] In the ensuing millennia, seismologists have made little progress in the search for signals that can more reliably forecast earthquakes. Changes in atmospheric pressure, groundwater chemistry, electromagnetic emissions, and the behaviors of snakes, dogs, and house cats have all been proposed, and later dismissed, as potential warning signs.

Similarly, reliable prediction of cyberattacks has proven elusive. Among other cybersecurity disciplines, threat intelligence, the cyber equivalent of seismology, is charged with predicting planned or imminent attacks. The focus of threat intelligence on detecting adversaries and their intentions and capabilities closely resembles governmental intelligence activities. The threat intelligence many companies collect, however, rarely suggests concrete action, such as making specific changes to cyber defenses to ward off imminent cyberattacks. Cyber threat intelligence is a genuinely challenging endeavor, in part because of the torrent of raw data pouring in from vendors, threat feeds, the dark web, social media, governments, and intelligence-sharing communities, all of which needs to be filtered and interpreted.

Though many cyber threats emanate from the depths of the internet and the output of cyber threat intelligence is limited, companies still have the ability to predict and act. The future of cyber risk prediction is already here. It just requires a change in perspective to see it.

Where Not to Look

Companies open themselves up to an attack whenever they change one of the computer systems that supports a business activity. All it takes is an update to a configuration setting or an installation of new software.

Tracking and analyzing the technical changes across a company's computing infrastructure is not feasible because of sheer volume. The process isn't useful because only the most basic cybersecurity analysis can be done without the business context that cyber threat narratives provide.

One area frequently mined for new cyber risks is currently available cyberattack techniques. From a tactical perspective, the cybersecurity group should be up to date on tools and techniques that facilitate the exploitation of system vulnerabilities. However, there is little strategic value in this line of inquiry because, as we pointed out in chapter 1, future cyberattacks are variations on ones that were understood and documented in the 1960s and '70s.

Another source of change that companies often examine for possible new cyber risks is large technological trends, such as the internet of things, big data, artificial intelligence, blockchain, and cloud computing. As is true of all computer technology areas, including old-fashioned ones like databases and graphics, they all have their own specific cybersecurity issues, and a company's cybersecurity group should be familiar with them. However, only in the context of planning and deploying a new technology will a company have the necessary detail to identify and understand how a technology exposes its business activities to new cyber risks. If anything, these trends remind us of the need to address cyber risks because of business's increasing use of technology to foster innovation.

Business Change Matters

Whenever business operations change, along with the technologies that support them, a new potential cyber risk is born. This realization provides a framework for meaningful analysis and prioritization. It also provides direction for capturing new cyber risks to incorporate into the day-to-day operations of the business. You can view a single business change from more than one perspective. Next, we'll explain how to appreciate these different viewpoints in the process of identifying new cyber risks.

New and Updated Business Activities

A business change that requires different support from underlying computer systems potentially introduces new vulnerabilities in those systems.

Adding new activities, such as developing and offering new products or services, can spark new risk. New cyber risks could appear in the products and services themselves or open new pathways for cyberattacks.

Changes in the ways a company handles internal functions can introduce new cyber risks, too. These changes can range from a new authorization process for procurement to the outsourcing of some HR or finance functions to a cloud-based provider. In procurement, the failure to properly design authentication and access control mechanisms to support and enforce the new process could introduce new cyber risks that expose a company to fraud.

Changes to Business Structure

Large-scale changes to the structure or organization of a business can introduce cyber risks. These include, for example, expansion into a new region or country. Most media coverage of nation-sponsored cyberattacks focuses on the sophistication of attacks aimed at targets in other countries. But a nation-sponsored attack can be even more direct if the target is within its borders. For example, in 2012, we brought media attention to the efforts of a few police departments in China in coercing foreign companies to install network devices that would allow the police to intercept all communications in and out of their China offices.[2] This case appears to have been a local initiative rather than a broad policy. But governments worldwide can gain access to the telecommunications infrastructures within their countries without having to resort to cyberattacks or on-premise installation of network equipment. They just ask for it. Or, as we described in the case of the Macau casino, even a competitor can have access to your information as it transits the telecommunications network it owns. We aren't saying that a company shouldn't expand into a country that presents new cyber risks. Rather, it should consider the risks a part of the decision-making process for the expansion.

Mergers and acquisitions can also open a wide variety of new cyber risks and consequences, because buying a company effectively includes acquiring all its current cybersecurity risks. The economic value of an acquisition can shift dramatically if, after consummating the deal, you discover significant cyber risks or breaches. If a company does not account for the cost of cyber risk remediation up front, then the pricing and commercial terms of the deal will likely be wrong. In addition to financial impact, a cyber contagion in the acquired company could spread beyond its walls to have an impact on the whole company.

Changes in External Business Ecosystem

The enterprises with which a company has strategic business relationships, such as alliances and supply-chain partnerships, are another source of new cyber risks. Third-party cyber risks are becoming more prevalent. Increasingly, business requires technology integration to support cooperation. Companies, in turn, have less individual insight into or control over the remediation of third-party cyber risks. The cyberattack on Target, for example, came through the legitimate network connection a heating, ventilating, and air-conditioning vendor had to the core of Target's internal network.

The cyber risks a company faces from its supply chain are more insidious than simply providing convenient pathways for cyberattacks. Vulnerabilities in the products and services that suppliers provide can compromise the computer systems with which they are integrated. The newly vulnerable systems could be those the company relies on to operate or power its products and services. Products as different as police body cameras, digital picture frames, and music CDs have all included malicious software out of the box.[3] Mitigating these types of cyber risks requires a combined approach that includes rigor in the suppliers' development processes and in companies' quality reviews.

The perspectives we have discussed so far all relate to changes driven by business goals and objectives, such as expanding markets, streamlining operations, lowering costs, or selling new products. For most, there are formal plans, a review process, and management approval. If, after your company has written a cyber threat narrative, a change rises to the level of critical importance, you'll need to be involved.

Changes Resulting from Ongoing Business Activities

Ongoing business-as-usual activities can also introduce vulnerabilities into critical systems. Sometimes they are the natural continuation of the changes we discussed above. Giving a strategic vendor direct access to a company application is a onetime decision that causes change. The management of accounts for vendor employees, however, is an ongoing activity that could precipitate a cyber risk by, for example, mistakenly granting more-powerful permissions than needed. Storing business information in the cloud is a similar example of a single change followed by multiple opportunities for new cyber risks. Configuration mistakes in file repositories in the Amazon Web Services cloud have exposed the sensitive information of countless organizations, including the NSA, which exposed details on battlefield-intelligence systems, and Accenture, which lost passwords and encryption keys used to protect customer information.[4]

Just as supplier-provided software applications can contain vulnerabilities, so can software developed in-house. Software developers seldom write programs from scratch, preferring the efficiencies that come from assembling previously written routines, some from external sources. For example, in 2017, the government of Estonia suspended use of over three quarters of a million smart ID cards because of encryption weaknesses in third-party software built into the brains of the ID cards. The German graduate student who wrote the vulnerable software had no malicious intent; he simply demonstrated the difficulties in designing and writing complex programs.

"Shadow IT" is employees' use of technology without the knowledge or approval of the IT department. Setting up wireless networks connected to the corporate network is one example. This practice has expanded dramatically and now includes broad use of cloud-based services and internet of things devices. Usually, employees resort to these work-arounds to improve productivity and convenience. Since they believe that the IT department is too overextended to deploy the desired technology in a timely manner or that it wouldn't approve, they go rogue.

Although none of these changes rises to the level of your attention, you need assurance that people have identified these under-the-radar means of introducing new cyber risks and that suitable controls are in place to prevent them. Keeping in mind that your company's own actions create new cyber risks will help you and senior executives be more alert when your company's activities, structure, or business ecosystem change. Before you plan specific actions, any discussion of cyber risks is hypothetical, but you and other board members shouldn't be discouraged from learning more about the broad cyber risk implications of business activities, such as establishing a joint venture, or technologies, such as the internet of things. It is simply means your oversight begins when your company is ready to do something. You don't need to try to predict the future.

Systematized Capture of Business Change

To handle new cyber risks on an ongoing basis, your company needs to embed the processes for capturing business changes into its operations. Similarly, your company needs to routinize the processes for how it analyzes these cyber risks and determines the proper remediation course.

Your company can start by looking for checkpoints in its existing change management and approval processes to capture relevant cyber-risk-related changes. It will likely need to augment these existing processes in two ways. The first is to expand their scope to include all types of business change that can introduce cyber risks. The second is to ensure that cybersecurity reviews are undertaken. Although many companies include cybersecurity reviews in projects that the IT department initiates, they often overlook projects that originate in other parts of the organization.

In our experience, people commonly assume that someone else is handling cyber-risk-related tasks, absent any supporting evidence, due to a combination of confidence in cybersecurity and IT staff and a belief that the task is too obvious and important to ignore. If everyone involved in planning a business change assumes that someone else is taking care of cybersecurity issues, then no one is.

All the risk identification, prioritization, and remediation activities we described in the previous chapter apply to the process of capturing new cyber risks. In addition, much of the analysis and findings developed when examining your company's existing cyber risks, such as identification of cyberattacks that can cause the most damage and the controls to mitigate them, can be borrowed directly from cyber threat narratives. In a similar manner, your company should draw on the same combination of corporate expertise used in developing cyber threat narratives to codify triage criteria as well as prioritize new cyber risks. These include personnel who participate in the day-to-day conduct of business activities and administration of the computing systems that support these activities, and cybersecurity experts and specialists in other relevant disciplines, such as legal.

Developing checkpoints is relatively straightforward. The challenge is deciding what to look at and at what depth; the volume of change can be significant, and it is infeasible to analyze everything. In the previous chapter, we suggested you prioritize scanning business activities based on how critical they are. These critical business activities are a good place to start since you'll never have enough resources to review everything, especially in a timely manner.

The processes and activities that ultimately enable companies to anticipate future cyber risks need to be internal. Only internal employees, not external consultants, can effectively know a company's operations deeply enough to spot brewing dangers before they emerge into full-blown problems.

From an oversight perspective, your job is to ensure your company:

☐ Captures business changes that can introduce new cyber risks

☐ Undertakes cybersecurity reviews of these changes to determine appropriate cyber risk mitigation

The aide-mémoire for this step is Fortify Inquiry 1 in chapter 12.

Know Your Company's Current Risk Posture

To meet your oversight responsibilities related to ongoing tracking of current cyber risk posture, you must ensure that the companies you oversee:

• Regularly test the effectiveness of their cyber risk controls

• Track progress on cyber risk mitigation plans on an ongoing basis

In order to understand and gauge how prepared your company is to face its cyber risks, you need answers to questions such as *Where*

do we stand? What should we worry about? What is in good shape?
Unfortunately, providing meaningful answers based on sound analysis
and fact is a challenge. The result? You get answers as vague as "good
over here" and "needs work over there" or couched in terms of the
relative maturity of individual controls. In addition to a sound basis
for the answer, your company needs a quick answer. You don't want a
process so complicated that the answer is out-of-date by the time you
receive it.

To achieve the goals of relevance, factual basis, and speed of response,
our approach leverages two ongoing cybersecurity activities: testing
control effectiveness and tracking the progress of cyber risk mitigation.

Testing Control Performance

Testing control effectiveness contributes to an understanding of current residual risk. This type of testing is essential because, as we've
shown many times, the presence of a control does not indicate the
protection benefit it provides. Testing control performance validates
how well a control accomplishes its role in mitigating a cyberattack.
In chapter 2, we mentioned that backing up computers is one of
the controls that would have helped protect organizations from the
WannaCry attack. Even as WannaCry essentially destroyed important
information by encrypting it, a company could regain access to that
information by restoring the relevant files from a computer backup.
Computer backup is a long established and widely used control for
mitigating not just cyber risks, but also a wide range of computer mal-
functions and human mistakes. In order to test the effectiveness of a
company's computer backup controls, it is not sufficient to verify that
someone is making the backups. One needs to go one step further and
verify that the backups can be successfully restored.

While third-party testing and reviews can help select specific products, your company should test cyber risk controls in-house. There are too many differences between third-party testing platforms and a company's own computing environment that can distort results. You should also not expect a control to reliably test its own effectiveness. For example, an anti-malware product can't identify the types of malware it can't detect. The first-century Roman poet Juvenal anticipated this situation when he posed the question "Who will guard the guards themselves?"[5] This principle extends beyond technology to cybersecurity staff. Someone who was not involved in making the decisions should review cybersecurity architecture and design decisions, such as embedding a car R&D network within a corporate intranet.

From an oversight perspective, your job is to ensure your company:

☐ Routinely tests the performance of controls in mitigating the cyber risks for which the controls were selected

The aide-mémoire for this step is Fortify Inquiry 2 in chapter 12.

Tracking Cyber Risk Mitigation Plan Progress

As we discussed in the previous chapter, a cyber risk remediation plan is your company's statement of the reasonable and sufficient actions it is taking to protect critical business activities. Once a company completes a remediation plan and puts ongoing cyber protection activities in place, the residual risk for critical business activities arising from that cyber risk have reached an acceptable level.

Before the company has achieved this milestone, the current state of progress on a plan for cyber risk remediation identifies areas of outstanding risk. For example, if the company has not yet deployed the controls it selected to mitigate a cyberattack, then the business activities vulnerable to this cyberattack are still exposed to an unacceptable level of risk.

By combining this status information with control performance test results, your company can give you a clear picture of its cyber risk posture (residual cyber risk) on individual business activities.

From an oversight perspective, your job is to ensure that your company:

☐ Provides status updates on the cyber risk mitigation plans

☐ Reports on the current cyber risk postures of its critical business activities

The aide-mémoire for this step is Fortify Inquiry 3 in chapter 12.

Optimize Effectiveness

To meet your oversight responsibilities for optimizing organizational effectiveness, you must ensure that your company:

• Takes into account organizational dynamics, interests, and incentives in determining the location of the cybersecurity group

• Promotes a culture of openness that encourages sharing of cybersecurity information and raising of cyber-risk-related concerns

Location of Cybersecurity Group

Creating a dedicated cybersecurity group under the leadership of a chief information security officer (CISO) is a significant step in advancing a company's cybersecurity strategy and defenses. The placement of this group within a company's organizational structure is an important element that helps determine the effectiveness of the group. One factor to consider is the alignment of interests and objectives between CISOs and their superior. CISOs and their group's activities should not conflict with their superiors' own objectives and incentives. Historically, IT departments have held primary responsibility for cybersecurity, so newly formed cybersecurity groups are commonly located there. This decision seldom accounts for the differences in mission and motivation between a chief information officer (CIO) and a CISO.

Broadly speaking, companies reward CIOs for deploying new systems and applications and upgrading computer and network infrastructure, all while accomplishing these tasks more quickly and at a lower cost than in the previous year. At a high level, CISOs are responsible for setting cybersecurity strategy and undertaking many of the cyber-risk-related activities we described earlier in this chapter. Fulfilling these responsibilities may affect some of the activities for which a CIO is rewarded and negatively affect a CIO's compensation if, for example, a milestone is missed. Beyond personal financial considerations is the issue of the CISO's budget and the cybersecurity activities, including the purchase of cybersecurity technology controls, that the budget can support. Since the CISO's budget is part of the CIO's budget, the CIO essentially makes the final decision between spending money, for example, to improve employee experience and spending money to mitigate the risk of some type of cyberattack.

We do not mean to indict CIOs; we have worked with many who have put their company's cybersecurity needs above their own financial benefit. However, sound corporate governance can neither rely on employees acting against their own best interests nor rely on the character and judgment of an individual who happens to hold the CIO position at a particular time. If a CISO currently reports to the CIO, the company should identify the controls that compensate for this inherent conflict of interest.

The decision on placement of the cybersecurity group should consider additional factors, such as the level of the executive to whom the CISO reports. While each company has its own unique characteristics that can influence the location decision, we recommend first looking at the CEO's direct reports. Having a CISO report at this level offers several benefits. The accomplishment of a CISO's goals and the success of a cybersecurity group's activities require cooperation across a company from employees who do not report to the CISO. A CISO's ability to wield the necessary influence to gain this cooperation is greatly strengthened by reporting to a member of the CEO's executive team. Further, placing a CISO and the cybersecurity group at this level makes a stronger statement about a company's commitment to and prioritization of cybersecurity than any memo or statement. This placement also facilitates the integration of cybersecurity activities and decision making into the mainstream of company operations, as the CISO is naturally part of discussions about the kinds of business changes that introduce cyber risks.

While there are generally no wrong answers in terms of which executive takes the cybersecurity group into their organization, some considerations can influence this decision. For example, given the ever-increasing cyber threats to industrial controls systems, and process automation in general, the chief operating officer (COO) is a logical choice. While an especially good choice for companies involved in critical infrastructure, it is also a logical choice for any manufacturing company.

When CLP decided to hire a group CISO, one of its questions was where to put the person. The decision boiled down to ownership of risk. Derek Parkin, CLP's Group COO, observed, "I am accountable for all of CLP's operations, and so both physical security and safety are in my organization. Yet, I don't have direct support in managing potentially the most damaging risk of all—a cyberattack."[6] That is no longer the situation, as the group CISO reports directly to him and sits just down the hall. Parkin sees additional benefits of adding cybersecurity to his organization through closer cooperation between physical security and cybersecurity and in extending the principles of safety culture to cybersecurity.

General counsels are another good option for heading up the cybersecurity group. Whether by nature or nurture, corporate lawyers are always looking over the horizon to anticipate future problems and then take action to mitigate or eliminate the risks that could arise. Interestingly, we have found that many general counsels have an easier time understanding cyber risks and their consequences than do some software developers, who are focused on creating new and useful applications and not necessarily on how someone could subvert their creations to cause harm. Chief financial officers are also a good choice. Their involvement in strategic planning and their focus on fiscal discipline are two benefits.

The final benefit for this placement relates to you and the board directly. As we've already stated, you and your board colleagues need accurate information for executing your oversight responsibilities. The further the CISO is removed organizationally from the board, the greater the risk of distorting his or her messages and findings on their way to you. Think of the childhood game of "Telephone," in which children sit in a circle and the first one whispers something to the next child. This continues through the rest of the circle until returning to the first child, who inevitably observes that the message just heard bears no resemblance to what was said at the beginning of the game.

There is one executive we don't recommend that a CISO report to: the CEO. While you could see this reporting arrangement as the ultimate corporate statement of cybersecurity commitment, the net effect is the opposite. This placement effectively cuts cybersecurity off from the rest of the company and its operation. It puts cybersecurity in a silo, just one that is higher up the hill than other silos.

From an oversight perspective, your job is to ensure your company:

☐ Has a rationale for the placement of the cybersecurity group that considers integration with the rest of the company, freedom from interference, and optimized communication with the board

The aide-mémoire for this step is Fortify Inquiry 4 in chapter 12.

Board Expertise

The opportunities for optimizing a company's cybersecurity effectiveness through organizational structure do not extend to the board itself. Essentially, boards don't need to change and can organize themselves, their committees, and procedures however they please, so long as they keep in mind the digital stewardship principle "Make cybersecurity mainstream."

Given cybersecurity's increasing importance and board members' general lack of cybersecurity experience, there are calls for enhancing their capabilities by appointing independent nonexecutive directors (INEDs) with cybersecurity backgrounds and establishing cybersecurity committees. In addition to the woefully small pool of candidates to draw from, there are several other reasons why this seemingly good idea of appointing cybersecurity-savvy INEDs is counterproductive. The first is the natural consequence that the rest of the board members will think they don't need to pay attention to cybersecurity because they assume someone else is handling it and will do a better job than they ever could. And, the INED risks becoming a likely scapegoat in the event of a breach. Cybersecurity experience is also not a good indicator that a candidate will be a good board member overall. The narrow perspective and technology focus of many cybersecurity experts mitigates against productive board service.

An INED with deep technical cybersecurity expertise could further blur the line between governance and management.

Boards should also not have a dedicated cybersecurity committee. As we've discussed, one of the most significant impediments to effective cybersecurity is partitioning cybersecurity organizations and activities from the rest of the company, resulting in isolated cybersecurity decision making, without adequate consideration of business factors. It further results in the mistaken impression that the committee is taking care of cybersecurity, so there is no need for concern. Therefore, creating a cybersecurity committee, a seemingly positive move, is actually counterproductive. The same is true of having cybersecurity be part of a technology committee, because it reinforces the idea that it's just a technology issue and something that nontechnologists can ignore.

CLP's general counsel and company secretary, David Simmonds, works closely with the board of directors. "Cybersecurity is not so impenetrable as presumed," he observed. "It is not just about high-end technology. It is a broad governance issue, just like a lot of other things boards do. We don't need to have a cyber expert on the board; actually, that would be counterproductive."[7] Simmonds continued, "The board views the management of cyber risk as a top priority and their cybersecurity oversight an important responsibility. Increased time for cybersecurity on board agendas and audit and risk committee participation in cyber drills are examples of this commitment."

There are ways to simplify a board's digital stewardship oversight responsibilities and reduce the time required to fulfill these responsibilities through organizational support. The aide-mémoires provide a collection of inquiries you can use as the basis for fulfilling your digital stewardship governance responsibilities. The aide-mémoires further describe and provide examples of the types of information and evidence that respond to the inquiries. Some of this information, such as prioritization of critical business activities, invites your feedback.

Other information gives you background and context that make it easier to understand the cyber risks your company faces.

Additional evidence confirms that your company has undertaken the necessary cybersecurity activities and has accounted for all of the relevant dynamics and factors. Creation of an inventory of computer systems on which a critical business activity relies is one example. While you need to know the company has undertaken this technical activity, there is no additional value in your review of the inventory. In this context, the internal audit department can assist you and the board in two ways that reflect internal audit's fundamental mission to assess controls and its direct and unique relationship with the board.

The first is by confirming that evidence, such as system inventories and cyber threat narratives, exists. This by itself gives you a huge increase in assurance in your company cybersecurity performance over what is generally available. Your company's inability to provide evidence in support of an inquiry could indicate that further examination of its capabilities in this area is warranted. In addition, internal audit can, on a prioritized schedule, assess the quality of the evidence and the processes for collecting and developing it.

Internal audit's assistance significantly reduces your time commitment and eliminates drudgery from your cybersecurity oversight responsibilities. It further benefits your company by focusing assessments on the activities most directly relevant to materially improving your company's cybersecurity.

Promote Transparency

Across all aspects of company operations, executive leadership needs accurate and timely information on which to base decisions. While getting this information is a general challenge, it is even more difficult in the area of cybersecurity. One reason is because so little about cybersecurity is immediately obvious to a casual observer. If you look at the Great Wall of China, it's possible to imagine the types of attacks it could repel. Not so with a firewall, whose protective capabilities are masked inside a case that resembles a stereo component. Even if you are not a professional house painter, you can still tell if a wall has been painted recently and judge the quality of the paint job. Not so for many cybersecurity activities, such as the configuration of a network intrusion detection server.

This lack of transparency means that corporate leaders effectively have to place more trust in the bearers of cybersecurity news. And to help ensure this trust is well placed, your oversight responsibilities include ensuring that executive leadership fosters an open corporate environment in which everyone shares and reports cybersecurity information, especially negative information, readily and rapidly.

To provide context for discussing factors that contribute to an open environment, we will first review some of the dynamics that influenced communications before and during a Singaporean cyber crisis in 2018.

SingHealth

The news finally arrived by email. On July 10, 2018, SingHealth's CEO, Dr. Ivy Ng, was informed that a week earlier, its electronic medical record (EMR) system had been compromised. In service for nearly a decade, the EMR system was core to almost all of SingHealth's critical business activities—from patient care to management to billing. Ng knew immediately that this incident was "very serious indeed" and directed the CIO to notify the authorities.[8]

Her instincts proved right, as she would later learn that this would amount to the "most serious breach of personal data" in Singapore's history.[9] SingHealth, the largest hospital system in Singapore, had now lost patient records on 25 percent of Singapore's population, including the prescription drug history of Singapore's prime minister, Lee Hsien Loong.[10]

Ng, a lauded pediatrician before shifting into health-care administration, still keeps pictures of children lost under her care in her office "to remind [her] that when we take care of patients, we can never do enough."[11] As CEO of SingHealth, this patient-focused sensibility translated into her clinical and administrative agenda, which included the security of patient data. Under Ng's watch, SingHealth made substantial investments in best-practice security technologies and processes having "approved all, and not moderated down, any budget request relating to cybersecurity."[12]

For years, a parade of auditors had certified the quality of her company's cybersecurity program, and the board's risk and audit committees were regularly briefed on cybersecurity investments, activity, and risks. The company had well-defined policies, in keeping with the latest international standards, and was focused on ensuring compliance with current regulations. It had a CIO who had a CISO as a direct report and conducted "phishing exercises on all SingHealth staff and email blasts to inform IT staff of security policies, responsibilities and security vulnerabilities."[13]

Yet despite these investments, trouble had been brewing within her organization long before the breach. The board and executive leadership had a limited view of critical issues and decisions that formed both the basis of the attack and SingHealth's response to it. Without leadership insight, decisions were effectively delegated to technologists and predictably reflected a lack of understanding of the critical EMR system and the business functions that it supported.

Despite Ng's declaration that the "horror of our patients' data having been breached is an unacceptable risk," the decisions made by

SingHealth's IT function did not reflect this view.[14] Years before the breach, in 2014, an IT employee discovered and reported the security vulnerability in the EMR system. Without a connection between the technology and the business functions, a midlevel IT manager elected not to follow up on it. IT later confirmed the attacker exploited this flaw.

In the years leading up to the attack, many security decisions did not reflect a thorough understanding of critical business functions or risk priorities. Security controls that would have thwarted the attack or allowed for an effective response were not implemented, even though this was a critical function.

During the attack, junior IT employees on the front line showed great initiative, though some of their actions were misguided. But management inaction at every level of the IT management chain, from the head of incident response to the CISO to the CIO, hampered the employees' efforts.

Evidence of an ongoing attack had been discovered by a junior SingHealth cybersecurity staffer months before the breach was formally announced, but these reports were stalled by the head of incident response who "held mistaken understandings of what constituted a 'security incident', and when a security incident should be reported." Further, he "delayed reporting because he felt that additional pressure would be put on him and his team once the situation became known to management" and was concerned that "it would not reflect well in the eyes of the organisation if the matter turned out to be a false alarm."[15] Further up the reporting chain, SingHealth's CISO "did not understand the significance of the information provided to him and did not take any steps to better understand the information," effectively abdicating the responsibility of deciding whether or not to escalate the incident.[16]

When staff finally reported the matter to the CIO, there was an additional delay in escalation and reporting to the CEO and the board in order to do more research in an effort to present a solution to the problem and demonstrate that the IT staff had taken the necessary actions to mitigate and contain the extent of the attack. That time had long since passed.

Amid public furor in the wake of the breach, SingHealth's board appointed an independent panel to examine the roles, responsibilities, and actions of staff involved, and to reprimand staff in the hope of "ensuring accountability" in the future.[17] As is typical of public breaches of this scale, the company curtailed bonuses, fired technical and security staff, and demoted the CISO.

In the end, both personal and organizational reputations were harmed, fines were incurred, executives were dragged through depositions and inquiries, and SingHealth was saddled with a five-hundred-page consent decree chock-full of technical requirements. SingHealth will be cleaning up for a long time.

Accountability or Blame

As the SingHealth breach illustrates, in the aftermath of a corporate cyber breach, there are intertwined calls for accountability and a search for someone to blame. Executive accountability takes a variety of forms ranging from angry stakeholders and legislators blaming the company to punishment through lost bonuses, executive positions, and board appointments. One of the motivations behind this approach to executives' accountability is to encourage their greater cybersecurity commitment in the future, not only at the company affected, but also at the companies whose executives watch from the sidelines. In short, the public's goal is to eliminate cyber breaches, and the approach is to hold executives' feet to the fire. Given that the calls for accountability come from outside the company, executives are not in a position to fundamentally change them. They can, however, anticipate the situation and prepare themselves and their companies should a cyber crisis occur, as we describe in the next chapter.

Leaders can decide, however, on their approach to cybersecurity accountability and blame within their companies. The choice is quite straightforward, even if it seems contradictory on the surface. They can either punish employees for their individual cybersecurity failures or have a company that is well protected from cyber threats. It is impossible to have both, because pursuit of the former guarantees that neither you nor executive leadership will get the information you need to accomplish the latter.

The external inquiry into personal responsibility that the SingHealth board commissioned after its breach appears, on the surface, to be a responsible and needed action. We can imagine the boards of other breached companies might wish they had done the same. The fact that the inquiry commended several employees for their actions under pressure could be evidence of the inquiry's objectiveness and fairness.

Let us look at the consequences of any activity that places blame and the way it influences human behavior. We have seen many cases in which the fear of personal blame has resulted in staff keeping critical information about cyber risks and vulnerabilities from company leadership. Several years ago, we met with the China managing director for a European manufacturing company for whom we had previously undertaken a cybersecurity risk assessment. He said how happy he was that we hadn't found any cybersecurity problems. We were taken aback because our report was far from a clean bill of health. The plant manager to whom we submitted our report had changed all of our findings to more-positive versions before passing it on to the managing director.

Even the mistaken perception that they could be blamed can prompt some staff to put a somewhat misleading positive spin on their reports. For example, the CISO and CIO for a large multinational company hired a cybersecurity vendor to conduct a penetration test of their network cybersecurity defenses, including the third-party security monitoring service they retained. To make this activity more realistic, they didn't tell any of their staff that this exercise was taking place.

Depending on your perspective, the penetration test was either an absolute success or a complete failure: the cybersecurity vendor was able to penetrate to the core of the company's systems without being detected. Even when the CISO instructed the vendor to make the attack more noticeable by doing the cyber equivalent of banging pots and pans together, it took significant time before it was discovered. Once the exercise was completed, the CISO and CIO convened a series of meetings to examine the reasons for the failures, create a plan to address the failures, and begin to execute the plan. Up to this point, everything the CISO and CIO had done was textbook best-practice cyber risk control testing.

However, as the briefing made its way through the organization to the board, the primary takeaway message on the penetration test changed. While making passing reference to areas for improvement, the briefing gave the impression that the company had detected and prevented the attempted network attacks. When we shared the backstory with the chairman of the board committee that received the briefing, he was surprised for two reasons. Obviously, he was surprised to find out that the results of the exercise were different from what he had been led to believe. But the bigger shock was why anyone felt the need to misrepresent the results. From his perspective, informing the board that the company had tested its network defenses, found them lacking, and was already in the process of remediation was a full-credit answer.

Fear of being a scapegoat closely follows the fear of being blamed and further discourages openness. Shortly after the start of our debit card fraud investigation at the Southeast Asian bank discussed in the previous chapter, one of the bank's executives said he wanted to see "blood on the floor," a sentiment he shared widely within the bank. One of the immediate results we noticed was that IT staff began lying to us. Even given the vagaries introduced by translation from Bahasa Indonesian to English, it was clear they had changed their stories from earlier in the week. Eventually they admitted that their manager had instructed them to lie to us because he was afraid that it would be his blood on the floor. His fear was ultimately unfounded, as he kept his job. The executive, on the other hand, did not.

Shooting the Messenger

In the 1972 Academy Award–winning movie *The Godfather*, Tom Hayden, the lawyer for the titular character, makes a business proposal that is rejected. Hayden immediately excuses himself and states, "Mr. Corleone is a man who insists on hearing bad news immediately." In this regard, the fictional Don Corleone is quite rare. The reason the expression "Don't shoot the messenger" exists is because this positive attitude toward receiving bad news is uncommon.

Over two thousand years ago, Tigranes, the king of Armenia, was engaged in wars against the Roman Empire. When one of his messengers told Tigranes that the Roman general Lucullus was fast approaching, Tigranes was so displeased that he had the messenger's head cut off.[18] And with that head, communications from the front line were cut off, and the Romans roundly defeated Tigranes's significantly larger forces.[19] The fear of a superior's reaction strongly motivates people to hold back some or all of the truth. One study found that 60 percent of IT staff do not report cybersecurity risks until they are urgent—and therefore more difficult to mitigate—and acknowledged that they omit negative details if they can.[20]

A related dynamic is incapsulated in the management bromide, "Bring me solutions, not problems." While this directive may have value in encouraging employees to go beyond the problem in front of them and find a solution, it is often counterproductive in the area of cybersecurity. The employee may not be in a position to fix the problem because the solution rests with nontechnical dynamics beyond his domain. As the SingHealth breach showed, fear of personal consequences arising from bringing a problem without a solution meant that staff continued to keep SingHealth executives in the dark.

There are additional reasons why negative cybersecurity news doesn't make it to company leadership, including different or conflicting interests related to the consequences of reporting the information. Consider a company that recently changed ownership. This company started as a joint venture between a state-owned business and a private conglomerate from a different part of the world. According to cybersecurity staff who were on the front lines of monitoring cyber intrusions at the joint venture, there were many attempts to breach the walls of the joint venture, but none were sophisticated and all were easily repelled.

The situation changed when the state-owned company bought out its partner and acquired full ownership. Soon after, the company's network monitoring systems alerted cybersecurity staff that several IT administrators were logging on to critical systems from outside the company's headquarters. Thinking that these administrators could be on vacation or traveling for work, the cybersecurity team checked door-swipe records and found that they were in fact inside their offices. This meant that someone was able to capture their usernames and passwords and then use them to break into company computers remotely.

This clearly indicated a marked increase in the sophistication of the cyberattacks targeting the company. Cybersecurity staff suspected that the change in cyberattacks was related to the new ownership. The country with full ownership has long been at odds with another country that frequently mounted cyberattacks against foreign interests. The new cyberattacks were consistent with the types of attacks previously attributed to that country.

A high-level government official who, by virtue of his position, represented the company's owner was about to visit, and the cybersecurity staff thought he should know about the new and more dangerous cyber risks the company was facing. They reported their findings, suspicions, and recommendation through the management chain to the CEO. However, the CEO had a different agenda for the meeting with his new boss and did not mention the cyberattacks at all.

Twitter provides another example of conflicting interests. Engineers at Twitter noticed that there were a significant number of suspicious accounts registered in Russia, Ukraine, and other parts of the former Soviet Union. Sensing that something wasn't right, the engineers recommended that the accounts be deleted.[21] However, the engineers didn't have the authority to do this. That power lay with the "growth team," a part of the marketing department, and that team didn't agree. Its primary concern was to close the gap in the number of users between Twitter and Facebook, and deleting the accounts would only widen that gap. The accounts remained in place and then went to work in the 2016 US presidential election.

In both these cases, employees had significant cyber-risk-related information, but no path or mechanism to communicate it beyond their corporate management chain. The company's leadership remained in the dark as a result. As these and other examples show, individual motivations and interests are strong forces that can undermine many different facets of cyber risk management. We have consistently found that blaming individuals is counterproductive. We further believe that trying to convince individual managers to report cybersecurity information that harms or interferes with their own interests is not productive. Rather, you need to make sure your company accounts for the human trait of self-preservation. Among other measures, mechanisms should be in place for employees, independent of their reporting structure, to alert you or a representative of the board about cybersecurity concerns that otherwise can't be escalated.

System and Individuals

In addition to preventing company leadership from getting critical information, blaming employees for the bad news they share neither is fair nor does it improve cybersecurity practices and defenses. As discussed in the previous chapter, a single control seldom mitigates cyberattacks, but rather a combination of controls working together. In a similar manner, the actions of a single employee seldom make the difference between a company repelling a cyberattack and falling victim to one. In the case of companies hit by WannaCry, it doesn't make sense to blame the person who didn't install the security update in time or the one who didn't back up the computers. If you are looking for who or what to blame, then you should look at the overall system of business and cybersecurity activity of which these individuals are just two parts. This is also where to look to make improvements.

The Agency for Healthcare Research and Quality's publication *Advances in Patient Safety: New Directions and Alternative Approaches* states that "the realization that adverse events often occur because of system breakdowns, not simply because of individual ineptitude," is the reason why many in the health-care industry are rethinking equating error with incompetence and no longer regarding "punishment as both appropriate and effective in motivating individuals to be more careful."[22] They realize that blame has a toxic effect. "Low reporting made learning from errors nearly impossible, and legal counsel often supported and encouraged this approach in order to minimize the risk of malpractice litigation."[23]

Companies should, instead, direct their attention to improving their systems and processes, of which individual actions are a part. A recent Chinese observation captures the importance of looking at the system instead of the individual when there are issues: "If all the fish are dying, the problem is not with the fish; it's with the water." The processes for identifying and mitigating cyber risks described in the previous chapter and the operationalization of cyber risk management described earlier in this chapter work toward strengthening and improving a company's cybersecurity practices beyond what it can achieve by focusing on the actions of any one individual.

From an oversight perspective, your job is to ensure your company:

☐   Fosters a corporate environment in which staff readily and
     rapidly report cybersecurity information, especially negative
     information

The aide-mémoire for this step is Fortify Inquiry 5 in chapter 12.

10

Lead in Crisis

Although avoiding and preventing cyber crises are top priorities, prevention only works until it doesn't. If, despite all best efforts, a cyberattack succeeds, your company must be ready with a response that both counters the cyberattack and addresses the needs and expectations of affected stakeholders, all while bringing your company fully back in business. Because of your company's previous efforts in creating cyber threat narratives and developing cyber risk reduction plans, your company can make significant preparations long before a crisis hits.

The technical response to a cyberattack requires a properly trained team, response procedures, and practice. Given its previous identification of relevant cyberattacks, your company already knows where to focus this preparation.

Your company's executives bear primary responsibility for communication with affected parties, the media, and governmental bodies. Each of these constituents has different priorities, ranging from attributing culpability to seeking compensation or assistance. Because of prior development of cyber risk remediation plans and analysis of consequences, your company can prepare for much of what executives need to say and the actions your company needs to take. Should the nature of the cyber crisis require your direct participation, you can use executive preparation activities and materials. Before diving into the preparations, it's helpful to look at some of the unique characteristics of cyberattacks and crises.

Characteristics of Cyberattacks

Crises, by their very nature, are characterized by uncertainty, incomplete information, and external forces that limit how leaders can act and communicate. Even if your company is adept at crisis management and accustomed to dealing with crises, leaders still need to address three core challenges of crisis management—extent of crisis, lack of visibility, and public perception—through a cyber lens.

Extent of Crisis

Determining the extent of damage, especially at the beginning, is challenging in any crisis. But cyber crises have one characteristic that distinguishes them. The geographical and organizational extent of damage from a cyberattack can far exceed that of other types of crisis. Social unrest and rioting may shut down an office or factory in one part of the world, but it won't have an impact on company facilities and operations outside the area. The TJX credit card case showed how a cyberattack that started in one place can quickly extend across the globe. The fact a hacker can attack at such an extensive geographical scale is a reminder that management's response to a cyberattack-induced crisis may need to address stakeholder issues across a much wider range of jurisdictions than a company is used to.

Predicting how long a cyber crisis will last is also extremely difficult. Given the lack of typical constraints on geographic scope and scale of damage, determining the full extent of damage and undertaking all the necessary remediation activities can take a long time.

Lack of Visibility

Cyberattacks are difficult to detect for several reasons. For one, they lack the visibility of physical attacks. The theft of equipment from a factory floor is both obvious and quickly noticed. The theft of the software that controls the equipment is not so obvious.

The start of a cyberattack can go undetected for a significant period. Recent analyses show the average time between a breach and detection, often referred to as "dwell time" or "time to identify," ranges from 101 to 197 days.[1] Why? Companies are not looking for the signals of a cyberattack, are looking at too many signals, or are looking for the wrong ones. Further, even if an alert is raised, it's not always obvious if a computer malfunction is the result of a cyberattack or simply the result of a software error or administrator mistake.

Also, determining who is behind a cyberattack is notoriously difficult because perpetrators can spoof all the telltale signs you could use to identify them. These include their location, the language used on the computer on which they authored the malware, and their time zone. For decades, hackers have usually first taken control of a computer in a different part of the world and then launched their attacks from there as a means of throwing investigators off the scent. Given the abundant marketplace for hacking tools and expertise described in chapter 2, finding a malware expert who can read and program in a different language is not difficult. The presumption that hackers only want to manage and update their cyberattacks during business hours fails to account for a cyber adversary's dedication, or the work and sleep habits of computer programmers.

Nation-State Attribution

Numerous countries are developing cyberattack capabilities, either on their own, as is the case with the US Cyber Command, or by purchasing tools from companies such as Hacking Team in Milan.[2] Some countries are motivated to use these capabilities to mount cyberattacks against individual companies.

Companies that are the victim of a widely publicized cyberattack might claim that a country was behind the attack as a way to deflect blame. After all, how could any company defend itself from such a powerful adversary?

Government agencies and cybersecurity vendors can benefit from cyberattacks attributed to countries by underscoring the need for their services and products.

Concerns over direct financial loss also come into play, as evidenced by the evolving market for cyber insurance. In the aftermath of the NotPetya attack, snack food maker Mondelēz International filed a claim on its cyber insurance policy with Zurich American Insurance. Zurich declined the claim, citing an exclusion for losses resulting from any government's hostile action.[3]

Public Perception

Many people, before they even finish reading the headline of a news article about a cyberattack, rush to blame the company instead of the hackers. The company inherits all the pent-up blame directed at poorly prepared companies that were hacked in the past.

Is this right? Blaming a company victimized in a cybercrime might seem akin to blaming a well-dressed man for being robbed, but there's a significant distinction. In the case of the robbery victim, he is the only one harmed. In the case of cyberattacks, many others are negatively affected through no fault of their own. Further, as demonstrated in the Equifax breach, which raised the risk of identity theft for over 140 million people, an individual doesn't even need to have a business relationship with the hacked company to be harmed.

People also tend to think that companies are lying about the true nature and extent of a breach. A company's own lack of visibility into the problem and leaders' confusion about what they should disclose and when fuels such distrust. That distrust can be further reinforced if executives act on information for their personal benefit before it is made public, such as executives' sale of Equifax stock before its breach was announced.[4]

Cyber Incident Response

Responding to a cyberattack, commonly referred to as cyber incident response, requires a combination of technical cybersecurity skills and experience in organizing and coordinating teams across an enterprise. The specific types of cybersecurity skills called for depend on the nature of the cyberattack itself.

Don't let the technical nature of a cyber incident stymie you. You can gain significant assurance of a company's preparedness by asking selected, nontechnical questions. Ensuring that your company is prepared to respond to a cyberattack requires assurance that your company:

- Assembled a team with the requisite skills and experience for responding to the most significant cyberattacks

- Developed cyber incident response procedures, with specific details on responding to the most significant types of attack

- Undertakes regular drills to exercise company response capabilities and identify areas for increased attention

Staffed to Respond

Typically, the core incident response team includes cybersecurity and IT staff. Though some common skills apply to any cyber incident, the specialized skills your company's incident response team needs depend on the types of cyberattack it will likely face. For example, response to a cyberattack that uses a virus could benefit from a specialist in reverse malware engineering. An expert in computer forensics, on the other hand, will be more useful in responding to a cyber incident arising from employee financial fraud. The cyberattacks and attack techniques identified in the cyber threat narratives help your company's CISO decide which skill sets the team needs.

Depending on the nature of the cyberattack, representatives from other departments, such as legal, HR, physical security, or law enforcement liaison, augment the core team. In the case of rare or seldom needed skills, it is often practical to retain a third-party provider. As a general rule, the company should maintain internally the expertise it needs frequently, while contracting scarce cybersecurity specialties only when required. Beyond these considerations, cyber incident responses that require deep understanding of a company's operations are best staffed internally. Activities that benefit from broad exposure to similar situations are better left to third parties.

Your oversight responsibility is to ensure that your company has in place:

☐   A cyber incident response team, with the necessary skills, to respond effectively to the most damaging cyberattacks

The aide-mémoire for this step is Crisis Inquiry 1 in chapter 13.

Response Procedures

The standard steps in responding to any cyber incident start with the determination that your company is or has been under cyber-attack. Limiting the scope of an attack and restoring the affected computing systems are other typical elements of a response. Escalation and coordination with other functions within your company, including emergency and crisis management, are similarly common activities.

Just as the skills required to respond to a cyberattack depend on the type of attack, some incident response procedures vary according to the type of attack. Response procedures that focus on the specifics of individual cyberattacks describe the associated activities and supporting tools needed. Before a cyber crisis strikes, your company should have both general-purpose cyber incident response procedures, as well as supplementary procedures for specific attacks.

From an oversight perspective, your job is to ensure that your company:

☐   Has the necessary cyber incident response procedures to address the most damaging cyberattacks

The aide-mémoire for this step is Crisis Inquiry 2 in chapter 13.

Incident Response Practice

Preparing for a cyber incident is one thing but quite another to calmly put into action. What may seem clear and straightforward written in a procedure can be challenging to undertake under fire. One focus of practicing for a cyber incident response is technical skill and judgment in activities such as deciding if recent signals and events indicate a cyberattack is underway or configuring networks to prevent further intrusion into your company's computing infrastructure.

Another aspect of cyber incident response that warrants focused practice is logistics and coordination. While perhaps not as glamorous as malware reverse engineering, practice is both essential for successful response and often inadequately treated. For example, if staff need to reinstall software on a compromised computer locally, you need to know where the computer is physically located. Cyber incident response plans often identify points of contacts for coordination and escalation by title and department. For minimizing the frequency of updating plans, this makes sense, but in a crisis it's essential to know the specific people to contact and their telephone numbers and be confident they know what to do when they answer the call.

We use the words "practice" and "preparation" to describe these exercises. We specifically avoid the word "test," which implies that you are evaluating or grading the participants. The purpose of the exercises is to identify areas that warrant additional focus. The exercises do not provide input for a performance review. Cyber incident response drills need to be sufficiently complex in order to test technical skills, decision making, communications, and logistics. A drill in which no one takes a false step and every response is successful does not improve your company's cyber readiness and is a waste of resources.

Ultimately, the goal of the exercises is to establish a well-founded confidence in your company's technical and organizational ability to respond to cyberattacks. By bringing attention to the importance of the drills as a means of identifying areas for improvement, you are setting the tone and expectations that will result in much more valuable drills.

From an oversight perspective, your job is to ensure that your company:

- ☐ Conducts cyber incident response drills and exercises that address the most significant cyber risks it faces

- ☐ Structures and organizes the drills to identify areas for increased focus and improvement

The aide-mémoire for this step is Crisis Inquiry 3 in chapter 13.

Executive Leadership

Cyber crises are business crises that materialize as a result of cyberattacks. That means your executives can rely on the crisis management systems and processes already in place. They can also utilize the materials already prepared to manage the associated business crises. Armed with so much process support, executives can zero in on the major elements of crisis management that are affected by the three characteristics of cyber crises identified earlier in this chapter.

What should executive leadership do or say in the event of a cyber crisis? Responses vary significantly depending on the nature of the crisis, your company's overall circumstances, and its cybersecurity posture. However, whatever the right action, executives can prepare for the situations and decisions they will likely face in the event of a cyber crisis. This requires:

- Prioritization of cyber crisis preparation

- Corporate-level decision making during cyber crisis response

- Directing actions to restore both the company and affected parties

- Providing information to the public that is timely, responsive, and addresses stakeholder concerns

Cyber Crisis Priorities

Given the number and variety of cyber risks your company faces, it may be impossible to prepare executives for all the potential cyber crises that could arise. To rationalize the process of prioritizing cyber crisis preparation, we recommend you consider three factors.

Significance and Impact

When looking at which cyberattacks to prep executives for, you should give the highest priority to those that threaten your company's most important business activities and would result in the gravest consequences. Since cyberattacks can damage business activities and a company so severely, you need to consider them differently than disruptions from other causes. Transmitting electricity across a power grid is a good example of a business activity selected on the basis of significance and impact. Loss of electricity, especially for a prolonged period of time, can cause significant harm to entire communities, and a cyberattack can have much more widespread impact than physical attacks on individual transmission substations.

Given that perpetrators can execute cyberattacks intentionally, executives should also account for the attractiveness of business targets to relevant threat adversaries. The cyber threat narratives your company has compiled for its most critical business activities provide the basis for this prioritization process. In particular, the descriptions of business activities, risks and consequences, and cyber adversaries address their significance and impact.

Cyber Defense Posture

Another consideration is how well your company is prepared to defend itself from different types of cyberattack. Deploying controls to detect and prevent cyberattacks can be a lengthy process for a large company, and the systems that do not yet have these controls in place are inherently more at risk than those already protected. Further, once deployed, the effectiveness of the controls can vary for a number of reasons. Staffing, investment levels, or the nature of the cyberattacks they address can influence how well a control can work. Executive leadership can consider reports on the current cyber risk postures of critical business activities for prioritizing postures.

Portfolio of Cyber Crises

Your executives face different issues and challenges arising from the unique characteristics of different types of cyber crisis. For example, cyberattack-caused environmental damage, such as occurred at Maroochy Water Services, and theft of proprietary software, as happened to wind turbine company AMSC, present executives with very different challenges. Your company can draw a representative portfolio of cyber crises from the existing collection of cyber threat narratives so executives can adapt to cyber crises without specific preparation.

Your oversight responsibility is to ensure that your company has prioritized cyber crisis preparation on the basis of:

- ☐ The significance and impact of cyberattacks

- ☐ The current cyber defensive postures of critical business activities

☐ A variety of different types of cyber crisis

The aide-mémoire for this step is Crisis Inquiry 4 in chapter 13.

Cyber Crisis Scenarios

After prioritizing the types of cyber crises your company may face, the next step is to develop scenarios executives can use to prepare themselves and the company, should a crisis occur. A scenario should start by outlining the business, political, and social dynamics that could lead to a cyberattack. This includes identifying potential cyber adversaries, their motivations, and why your company is a likely target.

To make the scenarios realistic, the description of the cyberattack itself should start by briefly explaining why an adversary would choose this particular type of cyberattack, as opposed to a different cyberattack or a different type of attack, as well as what an adversary needs to be successful. The prerequisites for success include the knowledge an adversary needs, such as how a piece of equipment operates, and the required tools, which can range from packaged penetration tool kits to a bolt cutter. In addition, the scenario should specify the location of an adversary, both geographically (e.g., local or remote) and organizationally (e.g., employee or contractor versus external). It should highlight the major steps in the cyberattack, all in keeping with the first principle of digital stewardship—"If you don't understand it, they didn't explain it." The scenario should conclude by describing the impact on your company and its operations and equipment, and on your company's customers and other stakeholders. The description should be compared to your company's risk appetite. Much of this information is already contained in the corresponding cyber threat narrative.

Your oversight responsibility is to ensure that your company has included the following information in cyber crisis scenarios:

☐ The broad context in which the cyberattack and resulting crisis could occur

☐ An overview of the cyberattack

☐ The consequences for both your company and its stakeholders

The aide-mémoire for this step is Crisis Inquiry 5 in chapter 13.

Executive Awareness

The information your company's executives need to lead the company during a cyber crisis includes an overview of the cyberattack, the cyber defenses your company has in place and why they failed, the consequences for your company and its stakeholders, and current progress on the response to the cyber incident.

While there will always be specific details about a cyberattack that a company can't predict ahead of time, the corresponding cyber threat narrative provides a starting point, with descriptions of the types of cyberattacks that could cause the crisis and the range of resulting consequences.

In order to understand the reasons why your company was unable to repel the cyberattack, first look at the relevant plans for cyber risk remediation, which explain the cyber risk controls your company chose to mitigate the cyberattack. Further, status on the progress of the plans gives information on where the company was on the path to acceptable residual cyber risk at the time of the attack.

No one can prepare information on ongoing cyber incident response activities ahead of time. However, your company can prepare to ensure that all the processes and sources of information are in place so executives receive timely and accurate updates.

The Fog of Cyber Crises

When a cyberattack started and what the extent of damage was are surprisingly difficult questions to answer quickly. This lack of visibility can impede executives' internal crisis management decision making and complicate stakeholder engagement. When it comes to cyber crisis communications, promptness and accuracy are diametrically opposed.

For example, US retailer Target first estimated that the breach of its point-of-sale system in 2013 affected 40 million customers, only to revise that number to 70 million one month later in January 2014. By the time the customer lawsuit was settled, the number was 110 million, almost three times the original estimate.[5] In September 2016, Yahoo announced a 2014 breach of 500 million accounts (a record at the time), only to reveal three months later that there had been another hack in 2013 that exposed 1 billion users. By October 2017, it revised this number again: all 3 billion Yahoo accounts had in fact been compromised.[6] Executives face the difficult choice of making early disclosures that can undercut their credibility because of inaccuracies, or of delaying disclosure and risking accusations of being uncooperative or opaque.

Your oversight responsibility is to ensure that your company is prepared to provide executives with information on:

☐ The cyberattack

☐ Cyber defenses and why they failed

☐ Progress on the cyber incident response

The aide-mémoire for this step is Crisis Inquiry 6 in chapter 13.

Executive Direction for Cyber Incident Response

The process for cyber incident response we described earlier in this chapter defines the technical and coordinative activities. However, some actions taken in a technical context can have broader implications for your company and its stakeholders. When it detects an active cyber intrusion, your company needs to decide how to proceed. One option, for example, is to allow the attacker to remain in your company's networks in order to collect more forensic information that could help in understanding the extent of damage and the techniques the hacker used. Another option is to cut off network connections in an effort to stop the attack. However, blocking connections to the internet could disrupt other company activities, either internal or customer facing. Should a company shut down an online retail platform or automobile assembly line when it has some evidence of a cyber intrusion? The considerations extend beyond the technical feasibility of the actions and require executive direction.

Given the inherent time pressure of responding to cyber incidents, it is important to establish ground rules for the technical response in advance. Your company should have clear guidelines on when it needs to bring leadership into the loop. Start with the supporting systems documented in your company's cyber threat narratives. The company should evaluate any cyber incident response action that could have an impact on the supporting systems in light of the corresponding disruption to business activities.

Your executives need to be aware of the potential business impact of cyber incident responses and approve of broad courses of action before a crisis hits. This does not require any technical cybersecurity knowledge. The level of detail we used above in describing the potential trade-off between locking a hacker out of a corporate network and locking out customers is sufficient and appropriate. The response to a cyberattack shouldn't increase the damage to your company or its liability beyond what it already incurred from the attack itself.

You also need to look at the broader significance of the response to a cyber incident, beyond technical decisions. For example, at what point, if ever, does your company engage law enforcement in its cyber incident response? The interests and incentives of law enforcement, including both police and prosecutors, overlap with, but are distinct from, those of a company that has suffered a cyberattack. While a company's primary objective is to recover and move past the crisis, law enforcement's objective is to find, prosecute, and convict the criminals behind the attack. Law enforcement could seize evidence or make public statements that run contrary to your company's own interests.

From an oversight perspective, your job is to ensure that your company's executive management:

☐ Has been briefed on the potential business impact of cyber incident responses and provided direction to inform decisions on incident responses

The aide-mémoire for this step is Crisis Inquiry 7 in chapter 13.

Restoration Plans

Before a cyberattack happens, your executives need to decide how your company will respond to the damage caused. While it may not be possible to predict the timing of an attack, it is possible to anticipate its damage to affected stakeholders and your company. These are described in the risks and consequences section of your company's cyber threat narratives and in a corresponding cyber crisis scenario.

As in any crisis, your company needs to prepare for repairing the damage, such as interruption of services or production, corruption of computing systems, or damage to equipment. Based on the experience and lessons learned from a cyberattack, a company can improve cybersecurity practices and controls to reduce the odds of recurrence. Corporate leadership, with support from the management teams and the cybersecurity group, can revisit the company's cyber risk tolerances.

In most cases, companies continue with the business activities affected in a recent cyber crisis. However, the Southeast Asian bank that suffered a massive debit card fraud provides a counterexample. Executive managers ultimately decided to exit the bank's credit and debit card acquisition business because they realized the bank couldn't manage the risks going forward. They based this decision not just on the bank's own cyber defense capabilities, but also on external factors, such as the commission structure in the acquiring merchant process that promoted fraud, and the lack of cooperation with other banks in fraud investigations.

The decisions executives make about the support your company will provide to affected stakeholders are some of the most visible actions they make in the course of a cyber crisis. During a discussion of executives' preparation for cyber crises, CLP's Lancaster stated, "Our values as a company must inform all we do in a crisis, and this starts with protecting life." Given the differences in the scale and scope of damage possible from a cyberattack, the activities your company undertakes for those affected may be different from those in other types of crisis.

While different types of cyberattacks result in unique types of damage, executives should consider a few commonalities when deciding a course of action, regardless of the specific cyberattack involved. One is the legal implications, including your company's legal obligations in potentially numerous jurisdictions. Also, setting precedents could impose future obligations on your company, should similar types of damage occur later.

Another consideration is the burden your company's assistance imposes on affected parties. Common corporate responses in the aftermath of personal data breaches illustrate this point. After a data breach has been made public, companies commonly send emails to all potentially affected individuals with instructions on what they must do to find out if their own information was included in the breach. Another common practice is to offer additional services, such as a year of credit monitoring, but this also requires affected individuals to take action to benefit from this service.

Imposing these additional burdens on affected stakeholders has two consequences, one of which is their negative reaction directed toward the company. Stakeholders can view a company's instructions as adding insult to injury. The other consequence relates to the effectiveness of assistance a company provides. If getting the recommended help following an attack is too burdensome, individuals won't do it. That means they will remain vulnerable to the risks the breach exposed them to.

Your oversight responsibility is to ensure that your company's executive leadership has decided on:

☐ The steps to restore the company

☐ The actions your company will take to assist stakeholders negatively affected by the cyber crisis

The aide-mémoire for this step is Crisis Inquiry 8 in chapter 13.

Accountability

While your company can decide how it will address cybersecurity accountability inside the organization, a cyber crisis can result in external calls for accountability, specifically in the form of leadership changes or financial penalties. Your company should anticipate these external pressures and prepare a response. In addition, it is possible to anticipate, and prepare for, the kinds of inquiries or investigations your company will likely face in the event of a particular type of cyber crisis.

The information provided to executives, as well as their decisions on restoration and accountability, provide the content for engaging stakeholders, which your company's corporate communications and public affairs departments can use as they would in any other crisis. The stakeholder engagement questions in a cyber crisis are the same as in any other type of crisis, even though the answers may be different because a cyberattack caused the crisis.

Beyond addressing these stakeholder issues, your company should consider two additional questions.

- Will public disclosure of certain information cause harm?

For example, if your company is currently under an active cyberattack, announcing it publicly could tip off the attackers and prompt them to adopt different techniques that could go undetected. In this case, disclosure undermines your company's ability to respond to an attack.

- Will lack of disclosure cause harm?

If your company doesn't announce a cyberattack it knows about, will it expose customers and other stakeholders to new risks they can't mitigate because they are unaware of them?

From an oversight perspective, your job is to ensure your company executives:

☐ Are prepared to engage the public in the event of a cyber crisis

The aide-mémoire for this step is Crisis Inquiry 10 in chapter 13.

PART FOUR

The Aides

The three foundation chapters describe the activities your company and its executive leadership must undertake in order to manage their cyber risks, promote the effectiveness of cybersecurity activities, and provide leadership in the event of a cyber crisis. To further assist you in your oversight of these activities, the aide-mémoires we present here give you specific cybersecurity questions to ask and the means to gauge the responsiveness of the answers.

By design, the aides do not address every possible corporate cybersecurity issue of potential board interest. From our experience, we know that there is a cost, not just in money, but also in time and focus, for every cybersecurity-related activity a company undertakes and you oversee. Resources, including attention, are always limited. Our process for selecting the aide-mémoires we include is based on over thirty-five years in the cybersecurity field across over forty countries, during which we have performed, managed, audited, or reported to boards on virtually every enterprise cybersecurity activity. We have chosen to address the most important and often overlooked elements of corporate cybersecurity. As we highlighted earlier in the book, many activities necessary for effective cyber risk management are frequently neglected because there are no market, company, or individual imperatives to undertake them.

We have drafted the aide-mémoires so that their use does not require any prior cybersecurity or technical experience, yet using them will naturally increase and deepen your cybersecurity understanding. And you can start using them immediately. The aides put you in the position of knowing the cybersecurity information your company should provide, as opposed to the more common situation in which a company decides what information it will give you.

Each aide has four components:

Inquiry. We framed the inquiries as questions whose answers should be in the affirmative or requests for information your company should be able to provide. We have written the inquiries so you can use them directly.

Rationale. A brief explanation of the role an inquiry plays in your company's cyber defenses and cyber risk management activities.

Evidence. Examples and descriptions of the types of evidence that respond to an inquiry. In some cases, evidence may also include guidance on how to develop it and who is involved in the development.

Oversight. Description of your actions to fulfill your oversight responsibilities relating to the inquiry. There are three types of board action:

1. *Confirm the evidence exists*

   The evidence in some aides is technical in nature, such as the inventory of computer systems on which a critical business activity relies. While you need to know that this technical activity has been undertaken, you don't need to review it. Given its role and its relationship to the board, the internal audit department could give you this confirmation and periodically validate evidence and the process used to collect it. If your company is unable to provide evidence to support an inquiry, you may recommend further examination of the company's capabilities in this area.

2. *Provide advice on the inquiry*

   Some of the aides address purely business and business-risk topics. Prioritizing critical business activities and identifying likely business risks in the future are two examples. Given the breadth of your experience, you are well suited to speak to these and other nontechnical issues.

3. *Be informed*

   Some of the aides serve an additional purpose beyond demonstrating that your company is undertaking activities essential to its cyber defense. They give you the opportunity to learn more about the cyber threats to your company. As the example of the Maroochy Shire crisis shows in chapter 8, it is straightforward to describe the connections between cyberattacks, the controls to mitigate them, and the business impacts, should these attacks succeed. Since we provide this information in the context of your board duties, your learning will be more effective, in terms of both the time you spend and the knowledge you gain, than you could achieve by attending a cybersecurity course.

11

Aide-Mémoire: Manage Cyber Risks

The purpose of this aide-mémoire is to give you the assurance you need that your company is concentrating on its most significant cyber risks and that cybersecurity investments focus on reducing these risks. This starts by prioritizing your company's most critical business activities and understanding how cyberattacks could cause risks to these activities. This information provides the basis for selecting controls and developing a plan for their deployment.

Identify Cyber Risks

TABLE 11-1

Critical business activities and risks

Risk Inquiry 1	"What are the company's most critical business activities, the benefits they provide, and the most significant business risks they face?"
Rationale	This question provides the basis for a true risk-based approach that focuses on specific risks to your company's business as opposed to generic risks to company computers. This is the first step in ensuring that your company's cybersecurity investments are directly linked to and prioritized on the basis of the business activities that create the greatest value.
Evidence	• For each identified critical business activity, a brief description of the activity, the value it provides, and the most significant business risks it faces. Consider activities that relate to your company's products and services and internal operations and concern your company's strategic future. • Meeting minutes or other documentation that identify the people involved in identifying these business activities and risks. These should confirm executive leadership participation in this process.
Oversight	• Confirm that the descriptions of business activities and risks have been compiled, in particular with executive input. • Offer suggestions on the selection of critical business activities and their associated risks.

TABLE 11-2

Supporting systems

Risk Inquiry 2	"Does the company have up-to-date inventories of the computer systems on which critical business activities rely?"
Rationale	Cyberattacks disrupt critical business activities by exploiting vulnerabilities in the computer systems that support these activities. In order for your company to understand the cyber risks it faces, it first needs to know what the systems are and their vulnerabilities. Further, the rollout of cybersecurity controls can be a lengthy process. Phased deployment of the controls should be based on the importance of the business activities they support. In the event of a cyberattack, the response team needs to know where the affected computers are located in order to perform many remediation activities.

Evidence	• Computer system inventories, including hardware, software, and machine location for each of the identified critical business activities. IT departments commonly maintain hardware and software inventories, though these inventories are often not kept up-to-date or do not include location information. • Description of the processes and tools your company uses to keep the inventories up to date and a few inventory update examples to demonstrate that the processes are in use.
Oversight	• Confirm that these inventories exist and that the processes and tools for keeping them up-to-date are used.

TABLE 11-3

Cyberattacks and consequences

Risk Inquiry 3	"What are the most significant types of cyberattacks that can cause critical business activity risks to materialize and what are the ranges of possible impact to both the company and stakeholders?"
Rationale	By making this inquiry, you are helping ensure that your company's treatment of cyber risk is aligned with overall business risk management and your company's risk appetite. The impact of a cyberattack is often greater than that of other causes of business disruption. Prioritization of risk mitigation activities and controls should account for these differences.
Evidence	• Descriptions of the most significant types of cyberattacks that can cause risks to critical business activity to materialize and the ranges of possible impact. There is an almost unlimited number of variations in which a cyberattack can be executed. It is neither practical nor useful to enumerate all of them. It is sufficient for your purposes in this inquiry that your company identifies basic types of cyberattack, such as an external attack that uses malicious software or an employee who misuses his computer privileges.
Oversight	• Confirm that your company has identified the most significant risks to critical business activities arising from cyberattacks and the ranges of possible impact. • This inquiry gives you the opportunity to learn more about types of cyberattacks and the extent of damage they can inflict on your company and its operations.

TABLE 11-4

Cyber adversaries

Risk Inquiry 4	"Who is likely to mount a cyberattack against the company and what are their motivations and resources?"
Rationale	Knowing the types of adversaries who are motivated to attack your company is useful input in determining the likelihood of a cyberattack.
Evidence	• List of likely cyber adversaries, their motivations, and resources for executing cyberattacks. These motivations may arise from specific aspects of your company, such as business practices, high-value trade secrets, or geographic footprint.
Oversight	• Confirm that your company factors this information into cybersecurity strategy development. • Offer suggestions on likely cyber adversaries and their motivations.

Mitigate Cyber Risks

TABLE 11-5

Prioritize cyberattacks

Risk Inquiry 5	"Provide a prioritized list of cyberattacks, based on the following considerations: • their capacity to cause risks to critical business activities, • the range of possible impacts, • the resources required for a successful attack, and • the motivations and capabilities of likely cyber adversaries."
Rationale	This list is a statement of your company's priorities for cyber risk mitigation. The framing of the inquiry ensures that these priorities are firmly based on mitigating the most likely and impactful business risks to your company.
Evidence	• The prioritized, descriptive list of cyberattacks.
Oversight	• Confirm that the list takes into account the four considerations identified in the inquiry.

TABLE 11-6

Select controls

Risk Inquiry 6	"Provide a list of recommended cyber controls whose selection is based on their suitability to mitigate the prioritized cyberattacks."
Rationale	This inquiry provides assurance that your company's cybersecurity investments address its most significant cyber risks and that the protection benefits of these controls are understandable in a business context.
Evidence	• The list of recommended cyber controls, including the cyberattacks each control helps mitigate and the business activity risks each control therefore helps avert. Generally a basket of controls, instead of a single control, is used to mitigate cyberattacks.
Oversight	• Confirm that the descriptions of the recommended cyber controls reference the associated cyberattacks and business activities. • This inquiry gives you the opportunity to learn more about the relationship between cyberattacks, the business activities they can disrupt, and the measures—that is, controls—your company is taking to mitigate these risks.

TABLE 11-7

Examine control effectiveness

Risk Inquiry 7	"Identify the measures the company is taking to overcome nontechnical impediments to the proper management of controls and the effectiveness of controls in practice."
Rationale	The effectiveness of even the most sophisticated cybersecurity controls can be negated if nontechnical dynamics relating to the management of the controls or employee behavior when confronted by the controls are not taken into account.
Evidence	• Descriptions of the measures your company is taking to neutralize nontechnical dynamics that undercut the administration and configuration of controls. Underlying causes can include lack of clarity on the intended use of a control or an expected negative response, should strict application of a control interfere with business operations. This evidence applies primarily to cybersecurity and IT staff. • Descriptions of the measures your company is taking to account for predictable employee reactions to controls. This includes situations in which the burden of using a control properly is too high or a control impedes work. This evidence applies to employees broadly.
Oversight	• Confirm that your company is addressing these nontechnical dynamics. If your company hasn't identified any impediments to control effectiveness, then it needs to look again.

TABLE 11-8

Develop remediation plan

Risk Inquiry 8	"Provide a cyber-risk-remediation plan that demonstrates how and when the deployment of selected controls, and associated activities, reduces the company's most critical cyber risks to an acceptable level."
Rationale	Beyond providing a cybersecurity road map, the cyber risk remediation plan is a statement of the investments and activities your company thinks are sufficient to protect its critical business activities from their associated cyber risks.
	The implication is that once the company deploys controls, develops related capabilities, and puts ongoing processes in place, these business activities are receiving the level of cyber protection they need.
Evidence	• A cyber-risk-remediation plan that, in effect, is your company's statement of the activities and investments needed to reduce its cyber risks to an acceptable level.
Oversight	• Confirm development of the cyber-risk-remediation plan.
	• Ensure funding decisions have been made in consultation with managers who own the cyber-caused business risks that the controls mitigate.

12

Aide-Mémoire: Fortify the Company

The purpose of this aide-mémoire is to give you the assurance you need that your company has the native capabilities to manage its cyber risks on an ongoing basis. This includes internal processes, with well-defined checkpoints and assigned responsibilities to capture new cyber risks and develop plans for cyber risk mitigation on an ongoing basis. It further provides direction on how your company can inform you about its current cyber risk posture and the implications for residual business risk. Finally, it addresses structural and operational issues that strongly influence the efficacy of all cybersecurity-related activities.

Develop Institutional
Cyber Risk Foresight

TABLE 12-1

Systematized capture of business change

Fortify Inquiry 1	"What processes and organizational support does the company have to capture changes that can introduce new cyber risks, including: • new and updated business activities, • changes to business structure, • changes in external business ecosystem, and • changes resulting from the conduct of ongoing business activities?"
Rationale	Tracking the types of changes identified in the inquiry is the most practical approach to identifying the modifications or additions to computer systems that could introduce new cyber risks to your company's business activities. Your company will only be able to consistently manage cyber risks on an ongoing basis if this change-capturing process is integrated into the routine operations of your company.

Evidence	• Change management documentation for all the types of change identified in the inquiry. The documentation should include the following information:
	
	  ○ The hooks and checkpoints for cyber review
	
	  ○ The (triage) rationale for deciding which changes need further cyber risk examination
	
	  ○ Follow-through for cyber-risk-mitigation action
	
	  ○ Assigned responsibilities and required competencies
	
	• Samples of notes, email exchanges, and so on relating to cases where cybersecurity-relevant changes were detected and remediation initiated.

Oversight	• Confirm that the company has change management processes in place and is using them to capture cybersecurity-relevant changes, and that it is initiating cyber-risk-remediation actions when needed.

Managing New Cyber Risks

The information your company needs to understand and manage new cyber risks is the same as described in chapter 8 for existing cyber risks. Therefore, your oversight of your company's management of new cyber risks uses the same aide-mémoires introduced in chapter 11. Since many of your company's new cyber risks will relate to existing business activities and supporting systems, it can use much of this prior analysis and documentation in understanding new cyber risks going forward.

Know Your Company's Current Cyber Risk Posture

TABLE 12-2

Control performance testing

Fortify Inquiry 2	"Provide test results that quantify control performance in mitigating the cyber risks for which the controls were selected."
Rationale	There is a significant difference between deploying a cyber control and receiving the protection it is supposed to provide. Through this inquiry, you help ensure both the soundness of your company's investments in cyber controls and the reliability of these controls to protect your company.
Evidence	• The results of cyber-control-effectiveness testing, including explanations of the significance and implications of the results in terms of preventing business risks from materializing. Controls cannot be used to test their own effectiveness.
Oversight	• Confirm that your company has done the testing and analysis. • Deepen your understanding of the connections between different cyber controls and the protection they provide to your company's most significant business risks.

TABLE 12-3

Cyber-risk-mitigation plan progress

Fortify Inquiry 3	"Provide a current status update on the cyber-risk-mitigation plan. In conjunction with the results of the cyber control effectiveness testing, describe the current residual cyber risks facing the company's critical business activities."
Rationale	This inquiry gives you an objective way to measure your company's progress in mitigating the most significant cyber risks it faces. In conjunction with the quantitative control-testing results from the previous inquiry and the previously established relationships between controls and the business activities they protect, you have the basis for truly understanding your company's cybersecurity posture and where it's heading.
Evidence	• Status report on cyber-risk-mitigation plan. • Incorporating the results of the previous inquiry, a statement of current residual risk for all critical business activities identified in Risk Inquiry 1, "Critical Business Activities and Risks," and projected date for when the residual cyber risk for each critical business activity will reach an acceptable level.
Oversight	• Confirm that the company has developed a status report and that it is timely. • This inquiry further helps you understand one of the most important questions you and your fellow board members have: "How well is our company protected from cyber risks?"

Optimize Cybersecurity Efficacy

TABLE 12-4

Cybersecurity group location

Fortify Inquiry 4	"Describe the rationale for the placement of the chief information security officer (CISO) and the cybersecurity group within the company. Describe how this placement considers integration with the rest of the company and freedom from interference, and optimizes communication with the board."
Rationale	The placement of the cybersecurity group within your company plays a large role in how successful it will be. For historical reasons, cybersecurity groups have often been established in IT departments, although there is an inherent conflict of interest between a CIO and a CISO. If your company's cybersecurity group resides in the IT department and it is not currently feasible to move the group, then you need assurance that your company is managing this conflict of interest. This is a governance issue and not intended as a personal criticism of any CIO.
Evidence	• Rationale for the cybersecurity group's placement in the company. • Measures the company is taking to avoid potential conflicts of interest that could undercut the CISO's effectiveness.
Oversight	• Confirm that your company is addressing this dynamic.

TABLE 12-5

Promote transparency

Fortify Inquiry 5	"How does the company foster a corporate environment in which cybersecurity information, especially negative information, is readily and rapidly reported?"
Rationale	This inquiry acknowledges many employees' reluctance to report bad news, especially if could reflect poorly on them. It recognizes that your company's ability to defend itself from cyberattacks depends much more on the swift communication of negative news than it does on touting successes. As a board member, you are uniquely positioned to influence your company's culture in a way that directly improves its cybersecurity posture through improved communications.
Evidence	• An official corporate policy on the importance of communicating cybersecurity-related information, with an emphasis on the lack of punitive consequences for employees whose nonmalicious actions may have contributed to a cybersecurity issue. • Examples of different types of internal corporate communications promoting awareness of this policy. • Organizational measures to ensure that the company follows this policy in practice.
Oversight	• You accomplish your oversight responsibility by posing this inquiry and confirming the evidence exists.

13

Aide-Mémoire:
Lead in Crisis

The purpose of this aide-mémoire is to give you the assurance you need that your company is ready to respond in the event of a cyberattack-induced crisis. This readiness includes both your company's technical capabilities to respond to a cyberattack and the executive team's preparedness to lead and communicate during a crisis. While incomplete information, uncertainty, and surprises are found in every crisis, the types of technical skills and resources your company will need and the decisions your executives will face are largely predictable and can be prepared well ahead of a crisis.

Cyber Incident Response

TABLE 13-1

Staffed to respond

Crisis Inquiry 1	"Does the company have sufficient staffing to respond effectively to the most damaging types of cyber incidents?"
Rationale	While there is a common set of skills necessary to respond to any cyber incident, the full set depends on the type of incident. This inquiry informs you that your company is prepared to respond to the types of cyber incidents that can cause it the most significant damage.
Evidence	• List of core cyber incident response team members, their roles, and qualifications. • List of extended, internal team member departments, their roles, and the types of cyber incidents in which they engage. • List of third-party incident response services, the types of cyber incidents for which they are engaged, and their contractual responsibilities. • How the company will continue to operate when staff are diverted to response activities.
Oversight	• Confirm that the information is provided and addresses the prioritized cyberattacks identified in Risk Inquiry 5 in chapter 11. • This inquiry gives you the opportunity to learn about the different types of skills involved in responding to cyber incidents affecting your company.

TABLE 13-2

Cyber incident response plans and procedures

Crisis Inquiry 2	"What formal planning has the company done to prepare for responding to different types of cyber incidents?"
Rationale	Just as the response to different types of cyber incidents requires different skills, they also require different types of response activities and associated tools. You need assurance that your company's cyber incident response team has thought through the types of cyber incidents it could likely face, understands the kinds of responses associated with the incidents, and has made the necessary preparations.

Evidence	• Cyber incident response plans that address the standard steps involved in any cyber incident, as well as additional activities that are relevant for specific types of cyber incidents.
	• Identification of the necessary incident response tools and how your company will have access to them in the event of an incident. Your company may have some of the more frequently used tools in-house, while relying on third-party service providers for those less frequently used.
Oversight	• Confirm that cyber incident response plans are provided and address the prioritized cyberattacks identified in Risk Inquiry 5 in chapter 11.
	• Affirm that your company has access to the necessary incident response and forensic tools for the prioritized cyberattacks.

TABLE 13-3

Incident response practice drills

Crisis Inquiry 3	"What types of cyber incident response drills and exercises has the company undertaken and what areas for improvement has it discovered? What cyber incident response drills is it planning?"
Rationale	Given the pressure and complexity inherent in cyber incident responses, it is clearly beneficial for your company to practice in advance.
	More importantly, the attention you bring to the importance of using drills to identify what your company needs to improve, as opposed to a demonstration of current capabilities, will make these drills much more valuable.
Evidence	• A plan for the cyber incident response practice drill that addresses the prioritized cyberattacks that can cause the most significant business risks and crises to materialize.
	• Cyber incident response drills of sufficient complexity to test technical skills, decision making, communications, and logistics.
	• Post-drill plans to improve cyber incident responses identified in the drills.
Oversight	• Attend cyber incident response practice drills.
	• Confirm that the company conducts drills for the most significant types of cyber incidents that could lead to a crisis and identifies areas for further improvement.

Executive Leadership

TABLE 13-4

Set cyber crisis preparation priorities

Crisis Inquiry 4	"What cyber crises has the company identified for executive preparation?"
Rationale	It is not feasible to prepare executives for every possible type of cyber crisis they may face, yet it is critical that they are prepared, should a cyber crisis occur. So the company needs to decide which types of cyber crises should be prioritized to prepare executives. By posing this inquiry, you ensure that your company is preparing executives to lead in the event of the most significant cyber crises.

Evidence	• Descriptions of the cyber crises selected for executive preparation, along with the rationale for selection. These rationales should include:
	
	  ○ The significance of the affected business activities and severity of impact
	
	  ○ Heightened risk due to lack of sufficient controls
	
	  ○ Portfolio of different types of cyber crisis

Oversight	• Confirm the selection of cyber crises and the underlying rationales. • Provide your thoughts on additional types of cyber crises for consideration.

TABLE 13-5

Cyber crisis scenarios

Crisis Inquiry 5	"Provide cyber crisis scenarios that describe cyberattacks that could cause a crisis, the broad context in which an attack could occur, and the range of consequences."
Rationale	In order for executive discussions on potential cyber crises to be useful, the scenarios have to be realistic and clearly connect a cyberattack on your company's computers with the impact to your company's business.

Evidence	• Scenarios for each of the prioritized cyber crises that include:
	
	  ○ The broad context in which the cyberattack and resulting crisis could occur
	
	  ○ An overview of the cyberattack, the requirements for success, and the steps involved in execution
	
	  ○ The consequences for both your company and its stakeholders

Oversight	• Confirm that the cyber crisis scenarios include the required information.
	• Use this inquiry, as well as the remaining crisis inquiries, as an opportunity to learn more about the cyber crises your company may face.

TABLE 13-6

Executive awareness

Crisis Inquiry 6	"Describe the preparations, including sources of information and assigned responsibilities, for keeping executives informed through-out a cyber crisis."
Rationale	Executives need timely and accurate information to both lead the company and engage with the public during a cyber crisis. Given time pressures during a crisis, your company should make preparations ahead of time.

Evidence	• Plans for informing executives on:
	  ○ The cyberattack
	  ○ Cyber defenses and why they failed
	  ○ Cyber incident response progress

Oversight	• Confirm that your company has identified the information sources and put procedures in place.

TABLE 13-7

Executive direction for cyber incident response

Crisis Inquiry 7	"Has executive management been briefed on the potential business impact of cyber incident response actions and provided direction to inform incident response decision making?"
Rationale	Some cyber incident response actions, such as severing internet connections, may have unintended consequences for your company's operations and broader implications for its stakeholders. Executive leadership needs to be both aware of this issue and provide direction. In order to avoid unnecessary delays in the response to a cyber incident, this analysis and guidance should be developed in advance.

(Continued)

TABLE 13-7

Executive direction for cyber incident response (*continued*)

Evidence	• For each of the prioritized cyberattacks, descriptions of incident response actions that could have an impact on business operations and a trade-off analysis comparing efficacy in resolving a cyber incident versus disruption to computing systems supporting critical business activities. • Meeting minutes, emails, and other evidence that a combination of cybersecurity, IT, and operational staff involved in the conduct of these activities performed this analysis. • Executive direction on business priorities to guide incident response decision making.
Oversight	• Confirm that your company has done trade-off analysis and provided executive direction.

TABLE 13-8

Restoration plans

Crisis Inquiry 8	"What actions will the company take to restore operations and assist affected stakeholders?"
Rationale	The efficiency with which your company restores operations and repairs damage caused by a cyberattack has direct financial benefits. The manner in which your company addresses the needs of affected stakeholders in the aftermath of a cyber crisis plays a significant role in influencing the consequences for your company's reputation. To provide sufficient time for reasoned discussion and to make the necessary preparations, this activity needs to take place well before a cyber crisis occurs.
Evidence	• Plans for restoring company operations and repairing damage to computing systems and equipment. • Descriptions of the company's planned assistance for affected stakeholders. • Documentation, such as purchase orders or contracts, showing that your company has made the necessary preparations.
Oversight	• Confirm that your company has thought through the actions it will take to restore affected stakeholders. • Offer your thoughts on the appropriateness and suitability of the planned restorative actions.

TABLE 13-9

Accountability

Crisis Inquiry 9	"How is the company preparing for external calls for accountability?"
Rationale	Fair or not, in the aftermath of a cyberattack, many different parties will assign blame and culpability to your company. It needs to be able to respond.
Evidence	• Plans for dealing with demands for leadership change. • Identification of likely inquiries and investigations and plans for response.
Oversight	• Confirm that your company has considered external reaction and demands. • Offer your thoughts on the appropriateness of your company's response to leadership change.

TABLE 13-10

Stakeholder engagement

Crisis Inquiry 10	"How are company executives prepared to engage the public in the event of a cyber crisis?"
Rationale	Through use of the aide-mémoire inquiries, you have ensured that your company has already collected and analyzed much of the information executives will need to draw on in order to provide company leadership in a cyber crisis. This inquiry gives you assurance that your company has used this information to prepare executive communication materials before a cyber crisis and established procedures and responsibilities for executive support during a crisis.

Evidence	• For each of the prioritized cyber crises, communication materials prepared before a crisis and company support, including updates on the cyberattack and response progress and the development of new materials, during a crisis, so executives can address the following issues:
	  ○ The cyberattack that caused the crisis (start with Risk Inquiry 3 in chapter 11)
	  ○ The impact for the company and stakeholders (start with Risk Inquiry 3)
	  ○ The reasons the company was unable to repel the cyberattack (start with Fortify Inquiry 3 in chapter 12)
	  ○ The plans the company has to address impact to stakeholders (start with Crisis Inquiry 8 in chapter 13)

Oversight	• Confirm that your company has done all of the preparations for cyber crisis communications. • Offer your thoughts on the engagement of the board itself during a cyber crisis.

Conclusion

At the beginning of the book, we made two observations about cybersecurity challenges most people are already aware of. Anyone who reads the news knows the rate and impact of cyberattacks are increasing, despite significantly increased awareness of and investment in cybersecurity. We've also seen many board members view cybersecurity as daunting because they rarely have relevant prior experience with it. The seemingly impenetrable nature of the subject only heightens anxiety for many directors.

The underlying reason behind both challenges is the same: the central focus of cybersecurity efforts is technological. The focus on software, networks, and hardware ignores many of the nontechnical factors of successful cybersecurity strategies. The technical nature of cybersecurity dialogue also alienates important parties and stymies cooperation. Jargon limits the material engagement that boards and senior executives need when discussing and making decisions about the cyber risks facing their companies.

In spite of continued inability to protect themselves, many companies pin their hopes on more sophisticated, and more expensive, technological products and services to keep hackers at bay.

Similarly, much of the advice dispensed to boards emphasizes the importance of cybersecurity training, and numerous classes and certificate programs are popping up to fill the void.

The absence of a working cybersecurity approach allows fear to replace logic. A fatalistic drumbeat in cybersecurity dialogue is emerging, marked by common refrains such as "It is not a question if you will be hacked, but only when" or the oft-repeated bromide, "There are two types of companies, those that know they've been hacked and those that don't know it yet." This spirit of resignation has shifted emphasis to reactive measures for dealing with attacks once they occur, rather than prevention or detection. This approach is the equivalent of neglecting seatbelts and airbags in favor of deploying fleets of ambulances and helicopters to ferry crash victims to emergency rooms.

Changing Perspective and Direction

You and other board members are best positioned to lead your companies in adopting a new perspective on cybersecurity that starts with concrete business activities instead of abstract bits and bytes. And conveniently, you can accomplish this change simply by fulfilling your oversight duties. Our digital stewardship framework gives you the tools you need to expand your oversight to cybersecurity. By detailing what your company has to give you in support of your oversight, the framework also tells your company what it needs to do to effectively manage its cyber risks. This entails a move beyond technology-centric approaches to cybersecurity and a shift in focus to nontechnical factors that are broadly ignored.

The responsibility chapters and aide-mémoires contain significant detail on the activities your company should undertake and the evidence it should provide. There are a couple of interrelated motivations for providing this level of detail. First, we want to make cybersecurity oversight as simple and straightforward for you as possible by giving clear guidelines for your company's reference and use. Additionally, we want to show your company what it needs to do to expand its attention beyond technical matters to capture the information and undertake the necessary analysis to protect it from cyber risks.

This includes giving you and other board members appropriate and understandable information. The first principle of digital stewardship states that you deserve explanations of cybersecurity you can understand. We wrote this not just to make cybersecurity governance easier for you. It also helps cybersecurity staff do a better job. If they can explain, for example, the connections between disruptions to a critical business activity and the cyberattacks that can cause them, they are in a much better position to know where to focus their cyber defense activities. And they are also better positioned to ask for funding for cyber defenses, because the benefit of the investments can now be clearly understood in a business context. Further, we want to show that all the activities that boards and their companies need to undertake for effective cyber risk management are practical and straightforward. No magic is needed or large armies of consultants. Employees who are deeply familiar with how their company operates perform these activities most effectively.

At a mechanical level, you change and improve your company's cybersecurity activities and defensive posture through your oversight requests for evidence. Put more simply, you promote this improvement by changing the focus of conversation from technology to the business that the technology supports. This change in focus not only improves the effectiveness of cyber risk management, but reduces the difficulty and burden on the board, executive leadership, and cybersecurity staff. For you and executive leadership, cybersecurity discussions and decision making are greatly simplified as a result. For cybersecurity staff, addressing nontechnical dynamics and talking with that affected people is much easier than many cybersecurity technical tasks. This change in conversation shifts attention from more difficult but less useful activities to those that are easier and more beneficial.

Stewardship for the Future

We have discussed how you and other board members are the natural leaders for your companies' cybersecurity efforts. But what about the broader question of cybersecurity leadership? Who can lead?

It is natural to look to governments for cybersecurity leadership, given their traditional military and law enforcement responsibilities. There are times when government agencies notify companies of external network attacks that the companies themselves are not aware of. But upon closer examination, governments are not well positioned to provide the assistance or leadership companies need. For example, they will never be able to understand the intricacies of cybersecurity issues within a company. They are also incapable of fielding sufficient staff to assist more than a small fraction of commercial enterprises, let alone the population at large.

The dynamics are quite different if you shift your view from governments to the commercial world. Companies like yours, and not governments, build, own, and manage the vast majority of the information, infrastructure, products, and services on which governments, commerce, and society at large depend. Companies are on the front lines of cyberattack and defense. The cyber protections your company incorporates into its products and services will influence how well the users of its wares will fare when they are under cyberattack.

Viewed from this broader perspective, the quality and effectiveness of your company's cybersecurity activities benefit not just the company and its immediate stakeholders, but the world at large. In fulfilling your cybersecurity governance responsibilities for your own company, you are effectively contributing to a safer digital world overall.

And you can start today.

Notes

Introduction

1. Matthew J. Schwartz, "Bangladesh Bank Attackers Hacked SWIFT Software," BankInfoSecurity, April 25, 2016, https://www.bankinfosecurity.com/report-swift-hacked-by-bangladesh-bank-attackers-a-9061.

2. Dan Goodin, "NSA-Leaking Shadow Brokers Just Dumped Its Most Damaging Release Yet," *Ars Technica*, April 14, 2017, https://arstechnica.com/information-technology/2017/04/nsa-leaking-shadow-brokers-just-dumped-its-most-damaging-release-yet/.)

3. Charles Cooper, "WannaCry: Lessons Learned 1 Year Later," Symantec Blogs, May 15, 2018, https://www.symantec.com/blogs/feature-stories/wannacry-lessons-learned-1-year-later.

4. Aisha Al-Muslim, Dustin Volz, and Kimberly Chin, "Marriott Says Starwood Data Breach Affects Up to 500 Million People," *Wall Street Journal*, November 30, 2018, https://www.wsj.com/articles/marriott-says-up-to-500-million-affected-by-starwood-breach-1543587121?mod=hp_lead_pos2; Tech2 news staff, "Aadhaar Security Breaches: Here Are the Untoward Incidents That Have Happened with Aadhaar and What Was Actually Affected," Tech2, September 25, 2018, https://www.firstpost.com/tech/news-analysis/aadhaar-security-breaches-here-are-the-major-untoward-incidents-that-have-happened-with-aadhaar-and-what-was-actually-affected-4300349.html.

Chapter 1

1. "Report of the Hospital Authority Taskforce on Patient Data Security and Privacy," http://www.ha.org.hk/haho/ho/hesd/Full_Report.pdf.

2. Berkeley Information Security Office, "Phishing Example: Message from Human Resources," https://security.berkeley.edu/news/phishing-example-message-human-resources.

3. Tom Reeve, "Even Security Experts Fail to Spot Phishing Emails, Finds Report," SC Media, May 19. 2015, https://www.scmagazineuk.com/even-security-experts-fail-to-spot-phishing-emails-finds-report/article/537183/.

4. Steve Ragan, "Malwarebytes Is Tracking Missed Detections in Traditional Antivirus," CSO, November 7, 2017, https://www.csoonline.com/article/3236254/security/malwarebytes-tracking-missed-detections-in-traditional-anti-virus.html.

5. Gerry Smith, "Why Antivirus Software Didn't Save the New York Times from Hackers," *Huffington Post*, January 31, 2013, https://www.huffingtonpost.com/2013/01/31/antivirus-software-hackers_n_2589538.html.

6. "Happy Birthday Brain, the World's First PC Virus," *Computer Active* 388 (2013): 9.

7. *Inventors and Inventions*, vol. 4 (Tarrytown, NY: Marshall Cavendish, 2007), 1033; Laura DiDio, "Antivirus Vendors Form Industry Regulation Group," *Network World* 5, no. 28 (1988): 17.

8. DiDio, "Antivirus Vendors."

9. MarketsandMarkets, "Endpoint Security Market Worth 17.38 Billion USD by 2020," press release, accessed May 19, 2018, https://www.marketsandmarkets.com/PressReleases/endpoint-security.asp; Technavio, "Global Antivirus Software Package Market 2016–2020," accessed May 19, 2018, https://www.technavio.com/report/global-enterprise-application-global-antivirus-software-package-market-2016-2020.

10. Geoffrey Mohan and Richard Winton, "In Sophisticated Shell Game, Thieves Hit Central Valley Nut Growers," *Los Angeles Times*, April 14, 2016, https://www.latimes.com/business/la-fi-nut-theft-20160414-story.html.

11. "2017 in Figures: The Exponential Growth of Malware," Panda Security Media Center, January 4, 2018, https://www.pandasecurity.com/mediacenter/malware/2017-figures/; Tara Seals, "360K New Malware Samples Hit the Scene Every Day," *Infosecurity*, December 14, 2017, https://www.infosecurity-magazine.com/news/360k-new-malware-samples-every-day/.

12. Private conversation, February 15, 2018. Additional detail on cybersecurity concerns during the 1960s can be found in Roger R. Schell, *Oral History Interview with Roger R. Schell* (Charles Babbage Institute, May 1, 2012), https://conservancy.umn.edu/handle/11299/133439.

13. Joseph Cox, "Hack Brief: Malware Sneaks into the Chinese IOS App Store," *Wired*, September 18, 2015, https://www.wired.com/2015/09/hack-brief-malware-sneaks-chinese-ios-app-store/.

14. William H. Ware, "Security Controls for Computer Systems," Rand Corporation (Rand Report), https://www.rand.org/pubs/reports/R609-1.html.

Chapter 2

1. Matthew P. Barrett, "Framework for Improving Critical Infrastructure Cybersecurity, Version 1.1," National Institute of Standards and Technology paper, April 16, 2018, https://www.nist.gov/publications/framework-improving-critical-infrastructure-cybersecurity-version-11.

2. American Chemistry Council, "Implementation Guide for Responsible Care® Security Code of Management Practices: Site Security & Verification," 2002, https://www.nj.gov/dep/enforcement/security/downloads/ACC%20Responsible%20Care%20Site%20Security%20Guidance.pdf.

3. International Organization for Standardization, "ISO/IEC 27000 Family—Information Management Systems," https://www.iso.org/isoiec-27001-information-security.html.

4. North American Electric Reliability Corporation, "1200—Cyber Security (Urgent Action)," https://www.nerc.com/pa/Stand/Pages/1200Cyber_Sec_Renewa.aspx.

5. Security Standards Council, "Securing the Future of Payments Together," https://www.pcisecuritystandards.org/.

6. Jennifer Bjorhus, "Clean Reviews Preceded Target's Data Breach, and Others," *Star Tribune*, March 31, 2014, http://www.startribune.com/clean-reviews-preceded-target-s-data-breach-and-others/252963011/.

7. Julie Creswell and Nicole Perlroth, "Ex-Employees Say Home Depot Left Data Vulnerable," *New York Times*, September 19, 2014, https://www.nytimes.com/2014/09/20/business/ex-employees-say-home-depot-left-data-vulnerable.html.

8. Yoolim Lee and Min Jeong Lee, "Rush to Take Advantage of a Dull iPhone Started Samsung's Battery Crisis," Bloomberg, September 18, 2016, https://www.bloomberg.com/news/articles/2016-09-18/samsung-crisis-began-in-rush-to-capitalize-on-uninspiring-iphone.

9. Jethro Mullen and Mark Thomson, "Samsung Takes $10 Billion Hit to End Galaxy Note 7 Fiasco," CNN, October 11, 2016, http://money.cnn.com/2016/10/11/technology/samsung-galaxy-note-7-what-next/index.html.

10. Robert McMillan, "Siemens SCADA Hacking Talk Pulled Over Security Concerns," *PC World*, May 19, 2011, https://www.pcworld.idg.com.au/article/387095/siemens_scada_hacking_talk_pulled_over_security_concerns/.

11. "The Black Budget: Top Secret U.S. Intelligence Funding," *Washington Post*, accessed May 7, 2018, http://www.washingtonpost.com/wp-srv/special/national/black-budget/.

12. Brian Fung, "How To Protect Yourself from the Global Ransomware Attack," *Washington Post*, May 15, 2017, https://www.washingtonpost.com/news/the-switch/wp/2017/05/15/how-to-protect-yourself-from-the-global-ransomware-attack.

13. Internet Archive, "Equation Group—Cyber Weapons Auction," accessed May 7, 2018, https://web.archive.org/web/20160816004542/http://pastebin.com/NDTU5kJQ.

14. The Shadow Brokers, "Don't Forget Your Base," Medium, April 8, 2017, https://medium.com/@shadowbrokerss/dont-forget-your-base-867d304a94b1.

15. Alex Hern, "NHS Could Have Avoided WannaCry Hack with 'Basic IT Security', Says Report," *Guardian*, October 26, 2017, https://www.theguardian.com/technology/2017/oct/27/nhs-could-have-avoided-wannacry-hack-basic-it-security-national-audit-office.

16. "Honda Halts Japan Car Plant After WannaCry Virus Hits Computer Network," Reuters, June 21, 2017, https://www.reuters.com/article/us-honda-cyberattack/honda-halts-japan-car-plant-after-wannacry-virus-hits-computer-network-idUSKBN19C0EI.

17. "SkyLock Product Description 2013 (brochure)," *Washington Post*, accessed May 6, 2018, http://apps.washingtonpost.com/g/page/business/skylock-product-description-2013/1276/.

18. Verint, "Our Company," accessed May 7, 2018, https://www.verint.com/our-company/index.html.

19. Jennifer Valentino-DeVries, Julia Angwin, and Steve Stecklow, "Document Trove Exposes Surveillance Methods," *Wall Street Journal*, November 19, 2011, https://www.wsj.com/articles/SB10001424052970203611404577044192607407780.

20. "Cyber Warfare Market Size & Share, Global Industry Report, 2018–2025," Grand View Research, February 2018, https://www.grandviewresearch.com/industry-analysis/cyber-warfare-market.

21. A zero-day vulnerability is one for which the application vendor does not have a security update, often because they are not aware of the vulnerability. The Shadow Brokers, "OH LORDY! Comey Wanna Cry Edition," Steemit (blog), May 8, 2018, https://steemit.com/shadowbrokers/@theshadowbrokers/oh-lordy-comey-wanna-cry-edition.

22. Internet Archive, "Webstresser," accessed January 18, 2018, https://web.archive.org/web/20180118144032/https://webstresser.org/.

23. Patching servers in a corporate environment takes more time and testing to ensure that critical business applications continue to work, and patching in an industrial control system environment may not be possible in all situations. The measures to compensate for these situations are, again, not sophisticated.

24. Kim Zetter, "How to Detect Sneaky NSA 'Quantum Insert' Attacks," *Wired*, April 22, 2015, https://www.wired.com/2015/04/researchers-uncover-method-detect-nsa-quantum-insert-hacks/.

25. Jacob Appelbaum et al., "NSA Preps America for Future Battle," Spiegel Online, January 17, 2015, https://www.spiegel.de/international/world/new-snowden-docs-indicate-scope-of-nsa-preparations-for-cyber-battle-a-1013409.html.

26. Wikileaks, "Quotation: Infection Proxy Project 1," accessed May 3, 2019, https://www.wikileaks.org/spyfiles/docs/DREAMLAB-2010-TMQuotInfe-en.pdf.

27. Bill Marczak et al., "China's Great Cannon," The Citizen Lab, April 10, 2015, https://citizenlab.ca/2015/04/chinas-great-cannon/.

Chapter 3

1. David D. Kirkpatrick and Ron Nixon, "U.S.-U.K. Warning on Cyberattacks Includes Private Homes," *New York Times*, April 16, 2018, https://www.nytimes.com/2018/04/16/world/europe/us-uk-russia-cybersecurity-threat.html?emc=edit_nn_20180417&nl=morning-briefing&nlid=5079423220180417&te=1 https://www.ncsc.gov.uk/alerts/russian-state-sponsored-cyber-actors-targeting-network-infrastructure-devices.

2. "Turkey Poses Cyber Security Threat, Holland Warns Travellers," Ahval, April 9, 2018, https://ahvalnews.com/cybersecurity/turkey-poses-cyber-security-threat-holland-warns-travellers.

3. Private conversation, April 16, 2019.

4. Scott Shane, Nicole Perlroth, and David E. Sanger, "Security Breach and Spilled Secrets Have Shaken the N.S.A. to Its Core," *New York Times*, November 12, 2017, https://www.nytimes.com/2017/11/12/us/nsa-shadow-brokers.html.

5. Crunchbase, accessed March 8, 2018, https://www.crunchbase.com/search/organization.companies/70fb49fd65d4beea2d65330825fd1023eed764a7.

6. Steve Morgan, "Hackerpocalypse: A Cybercrime Revelation," Cybersecurity Ventures, August 26, 2016, https://cybersecurityventures.com/hackerpocalypse-original-cybercrime-report-2016/.

7. "2018 CrowdStrike Global Threat Report: Blurring the Lines Between Statecraft and Tradecraft," CrowdStrike, 2018, https://www.crowdstrike.com/resources/reports/2018-crowdstrike-global-threat-report-blurring-the-lines-between-statecraft-and-tradecraft/.

8. United States Senate Committee on Commerce, Science, and Transportation, Hearing on Improving Cybersecurity, statement of Edward Amoroso, Senior Vice President and Chief Security Officer of AT&T, March 19, 2009, https://www.commerce.senate.gov/public/_cache/files/e8d018c6-bf5f-4ea6-9ecc-a990c4b954c4/750D7CB7E272E1FE44016EA5F7A503D2.testimonyofedamoroso31709.pdf.

9. AT&T net income in the year of Amoroso's testimony was $12.5 million. AT&T Inc., 2009 Annual Report, December 31, 2009, p. 30, accessed March 9, 2018, https://www.att.com/Common/about_us/annual_report/pdfs/ATT2009_Financials.pdf.

10. In 2009, $1 trillion would place cybercrime as the thirteenth largest GDP out of 183 countries. International Monetary Fund, "World Economic Outlook Database," April 2012 edition, http://www.imf.org/external/pubs/ft/weo/2012/01/weodata/index.aspx.

11. "NYS Legislature Hosts Distracted Driving Lobby Day Event," YouTube video, 46:05, posted by NYSenate, April 24, 2017, https://www.youtube.com/watch?v=r3N0TL_WEtE.

12. Senate Bill S6325A, Sess. of 2015-2016 (NY 2016), http://legislation.
nysenate.gov/pdf/bills/2015/S6325A; Insurance Institute for Highway Safety,
"Cellphone Use Laws by State," accessed July 17, 2019, https://www.iihs.org/
topics/distracted-driving/cellphone-use-laws; police reported crashes in 2015:
US Department of Transportation's National Center for Statistics and Analysis
(NCSA) Motor Vehicle Traffic Crash Data Resource Page, "Quick Facts 2016,"
https://crashstats.nhtsa.dot.gov/Api/Public/ViewPublication/812451.

13. US Department of Justice, Office of Justice Programs, "Census of State
and Local Law Enforcement Agencies, 2008," July 2011, https://www.bjs.gov/
content/pub/pdf/csllea08.pdf; "Distracted Operators Risk Casualties (DORCs):
New York State Legislature and DORCs Announce Unique Efforts to Combat
Distracted Driving," PR Newswire, April 5, 2016, https://www.prnewswire.
com/news-releases/new-york-state-legislature-and-dorcs-announce-unique-
efforts-to-combat-distracted-driving-300246450.html.

14. Lobbying issues include "Issues related to criminal justice, national
security, homeland security, and digital evidence and forensics," US Senate
Lobbying Disclosure Act Database, "LD-2 Disclosure Form," accessed March 9,
2018, https://soprweb.senate.gov/index.cfm?event=getFilingDetails&filingID=1D
E19BE9-5152-4AB3-8037-D7194268FD0B&filingTypeID=51.

15. E-ISAC and SANS ICS report, "Analysis of the Cyber Attack on the
Ukrainian Power Grid," March 18, 2016, p. 4, http://www.nerc.com/pa/CI/
ESISAC/Documents/E-ISAC_SANS_Ukraine_DUC_18Mar2016.pdf.

16. Kim Zetter, "Hackers Finally Post Stolen Ashley Madison Data," *Wired*,
August 18, 2015, https://www.wired.com/2015/08/happened-hackers-posted-
stolen-ashley-madison-data/.

17. Troy Mursch, "Large Cryptojacking Campaign Targeting Vulnerable
Drupal Websites," Bad Packets Report, May 5, 2018, https://badpackets.net/
large-cryptojacking-campaign-targeting-vulnerable-drupal-websites/.

18. Brian Fung, "Equifax's Massive 2017 Data Breach Keeps Getting Worse,"
Washington Post, March 1, 2018, https://www.washingtonpost.com/news/the-
switch/wp/2018/03/01/equifax-keeps-finding-millions-more-people-who-were-
affected-by-its-massive-data-breach/.

Chapter 5

1. Thomas Parenty, *Digital Defense: What You Should Know About Protecting
Your Company's Assets* (Boston: Harvard Business School Press, 2003), xvii.

2. Ibid., 23.

Chapter 7

1. Steven Kerr, "On the Folly of Rewarding A, While Hoping for B,"
Academy of Management Executive 9, no. 1 (February 1995), accessed December 15,
2018, https://www.ou.edu/russell/UGcomp/Kerr.pdf.

Chapter 8

1. Private conversation, May 20, 2019.

2. Macau Gaming Inspection and Coordination Bureau, accessed January 17, 2019, http://www.dicj.gov.mo/web/en/information/DadosEstat/index.html.

3. A. Shameen, "Think Southeast Asia Is Taking a Backseat? Think Again," *Chief Executive* 217 (2006): 44–47.

4. Brigid Sweeney, "The Frightening New Frontier for Hackers: Medical Records," *Modern Healthcare*, April 10, 2017, https://www.modernhealthcare.com/article/20170410/NEWS/170419987.

5. K. J. Biba, "Integrity Considerations for Secure Computer Systems," MITRE technical report, June 30, 1975, http://seclab.cs.ucdavis.edu/projects/history/papers/biba75.pdf.

6. United States of America v. Albert Gonzalez et al., 08 CR 10.2.2.3 PBS (US District Court of Massachusetts, 2008).

7. E-ISAC and SANS ICS report, "Analysis of the Cyber Attack on the Ukrainian Power Grid," March 18, 2016, p. 4, http://www.nerc.com/pa/CI/ESISAC/Documents/E-ISAC_SANS_Ukraine_DUC_18Mar2016.pdf; Kim Zetter, "Inside the Cunning, Unprecedented Hack of Ukraine's Power Grid," *Wired*, March 3, 2016, https://www.wired.com/2016/03/inside-cunning-unprecedented-hack-ukraines-power-grid/.

8. Joe Slowik, "Anatomy of an Attack: Detecting and Defeating CRASHOVERRIDE," Dragos white paper, accessed December 3, 2018, https://dragos.com/whitepapers/CrashOverride2018.html.

9. Owen Hughes, "WannaCry Impact on NHS Considerably Larger Than Previously Suggested," Digital Health, October 27, 2017, https://www.digitalhealth.net/2017/10/wannacry-impact-on-nhs-considerably-larger-than-previously-suggested/.

10. Richard Milne, "Moller-Maersk Puts Cost of Cyber Attack at Up to $300m," *Financial Times*, August 16, 2017, https://www.ft.com/content/a44ede7c-825f-11e7-a4ce-15b2513cb3ff; Kim S. Nash, Sarah Castellanos, and Adam Janofsky, "One Year After NotPetya Cyberattack, Firms Wrestle with Recovery Costs," *Wall Street Journal*, June 27, 2018, https://www.wsj.com/articles/one-year-after-notpetya-companies-still-wrestle-with-financial-impacts-1530095906.

11. Ibid.

12. Bill Berkrot, "Merck Keytruda Sales Soar, But European Application Pulled," Reuters, October 27, 2017, https://www.reuters.com/article/us-merck-co-results/merck-keytruda-sales-soar-but-european-application-pulled-idUSKBN1CW1EF; Centers for Disease Control and Prevention, accessed February 3, 2019, https://www.cdc.gov/hpv/parents/questions-answers.html.

13. Nate Raymond, "China's Sinovel Convicted in U.S. of Trade-Secret Theft," Reuters, January 24, 2018, https://www.reuters.com/article/us-sinovel-wind-gro-usa-court/chinas-sinovel-convicted-in-u-s-of-trade-secret-theft-idUSKBN1FD2XL.

14. AMSC annual reports, accessed December 2, 2018, https://ir.amsc.com/financial-information/annual-reports.

15. Barton Gellman and Jerry Markon, "Edward Snowden Says Motive Behind Leaks Was to Expose 'Surveillance State,'" *Washington Post*, June 10, 2013, https://wapo.st/31Gc1jd.

16. Kim Zetter, "Oil Companies Spring a Leak, Courtesy of Anonymous," *Wired*, July 16, 2012, https://www.wired.com/2012/07/oil-companies-hacked/.

17. Bloomberg, "MedSec's CEO: St Jude Has History of Sweeping Things Under Table," YouTube, August 25, 2016, https://www.youtube.com/watch?v=curdJoTysF8.

18. Tom Spring, "Researchers: MedSec, Muddy Waters Set Bad Precedent with St. Jude Medical Short," Threatpost, August 31, 2016, https://threatpost.com/researchers-medsec-muddy-waters-set-bad-precedent-with-st-jude-medical-short/120266/.

19. Reuters, "Medical Supplier St. Jude Is Suing Short Seller Muddy Waters," Fortune.com, September 7, 2016, http://fortune.com/2016/09/07/st-jude-sues-muddy-waters/.

20. U.S. Food and Drug Administration, "Firmware Update to Address Cybersecurity Vulnerabilities Identified in Abbott's Implantable Cardiac Pacemakers: FDA Safety Communication," August 29, 2017, https://www.fda.gov/MedicalDevices/Safety/AlertsandNotices/ucm573669.

21. Joseph Weiss, *Protecting Industrial Control Systems from Electronic Threats* (New York: Momentum Press, 2010), 109.

22. Nabil Sayfayn and Stuart Madnick, "Safety Analysis of the Maroochy Shire Sewage Spill," working paper, MIT Sloan School of Management, May 2017, http://web.mit.edu/smadnick/www/wp/2017-09.pdf.

23. Cornelia Dean, "Indulged on Australia's Sunshine Coast," *New York Times*, April 4, 1993, https://www.nytimes.com/1993/04/04/travel/indulged-on-australia-s-sunshine-coast.html.

24. Glenis Green, "Hacker Caused Sewage Overflows, Court Told," *Courier-Mail,* October 17, 2001, https://www.mail-archive.com/cybercrime-alerts@topica.com/msg00577.html.

25. Ibid.

26. Glenis Green, "Hacker Jailed for Sewage Sabotage" *Courier-Mail*, November 1, 2001, http://web.mit.edu/smadnick/www/wp/2017-09.pdf.

27. "Information technology—Security techniques—Code of practice for information security controls/*Technologies de l'information—Techniques de sécurité—Code de bonne pratique pour le management de la sécurité de l'information*," ISO (International Organization for Standardization) and IEC (International Electrotechnical Commission), Geneva, Switzerland, 2013.

28. Mary K. Pratt, "What Is SIEM Software? How It Works and How to Choose the Right Tool," CSO.com, November 28, 2017, https://www.csoonline.

com/article/2124604/network-security/what-is-siem-software-how-it-works-and-how-to-choose-the-right-tool.html.

29. Michael Riley, Ben Elgin, Dune Lawrence, and Carol Matlack, "Missed Alarms and 40 Million Stolen Credit Card Numbers: How Target Blew It," *Bloomberg Businessweek*, March 17, 2014, https://www.bloomberg.com/news/articles/2014-03-13/target-missed-warnings-in-epic-hack-of-credit-card-data.

30. Elizabeth A. Harris and Nicole Perlroth, "Target Missed Signs of a Data Breach," *New York Times*, March 13, 2014, https://www.nytimes.com/2014/03/14/business/target-missed-signs-of-a-data-breach.html.

31. Excavations of ancient Babylon uncovered cylinders with inscriptions for making soap around 2800 BCE.

32. C. Borchgrevink, J. Cha, and S. Kim, "Hand Washing Practices in a College Town Environment," *Journal of Environmental Health* 75, no. 8 (2013): 18–24.

33. M. Mazurek et al., "Measuring Password Guessability for an Entire University," working paper, Carnegie Mellon Cylab, October 22, 2013, https://www.cylab.cmu.edu/_files/pdfs/tech_reports/CMUCyLab13013.pdf.

Chapter 9

1. Aristotle, *Meteorology*, trans. E. W. Webster, Internet Classics Archive, accessed January 17, 2019, http://classics.mit.edu/Aristotle/meteorology.2.ii.html.

2. Kevin Voight, "International Firms Caught in China's Security Web," CNN, August 24, 2012, https://www.cnn.com/2012/08/24/business/china-foreign-companies-internet/index.html; Jonathan Ansfield, "Chinese Authorities Putting Pressure on Businesses to Help Censor the Web," *New York Times*, November 13, 2012, https://www.nytimes.com/2012/11/14/world/asia/china-pressures-businesses-to-help-censor-web.html.

3. Catalin Cimpanu, "Police Body Cameras Shipped with Pre-Installed Conficker Virus," Softpedia News, November 15, 2015, https://news.softpedia.com/news/police-body-cameras-shipped-with-pre-installed-conficker-virus-496177.shtml; Gregg Keizer, "Best Buy Sold Infected Digital Picture Frames," *Computerworld*, January 23, 2008, https://www.computerworld.com/article/2538961/best-buy-sold-infected-digital-picture-frames.html; Bruce Schneier, "Real Story of the Rogue Rootkit," *Wired*, November 5, 2017, https://www.wired.com/2005/11/real-story-of-the-rogue-rootkit/.

4. "Classified Pentagon Data Leaked on the Public Cloud," BBC News, November 29, 2017, https://www.bbc.com/news/technology-42166004; Zack Whittaker, "Accenture Left a Huge Trove of Highly Sensitive Data on Exposed Servers," ZDNet, October 10, 2017, https://www.zdnet.com/article/accenture-left-a-huge-trove-of-client-passwords-on-exposed-servers/.

5. Wikipedia, accessed January 23, 2019, https://en.wikipedia.org/wiki/Quis_custodiet_ipsos_custodes%3F.

6. Private conversation, May 17, 2019.

7. Ibid.

8. Singapore Ministry of Communications and Information, "Public Report of the Committee of Inquiry (COI) into the Cyber-attack on Singapore Health Services Private Limited Patient Database," press release, accessed March 6, 2019, https://www.mci.gov.sg/pressroom/news-and-stories/pressroom/2019/1/public-report-of-the-coi.

9. Statement at Parliament by S. Iswaran, minister in charge of cybersecurity, on the cyberattack on SingHealth's IT system, August 6, 2018.

10. Ibid.

11. "Why SingHealth CEO Keeps Photos of Dead Young Patients in Her Office," AsiaOne, accessed March 5, 2019, https://www.asiaone.com/health/why-singhealth-ceo-keeps-photos-of-dead-young-patients-her-office.

12. Singapore Ministry of Communications and Information, "Public Report of the Committee of Inquiry," p. 15.

13. Channel NewsAsia, "SingHealth COI Report: 16 Recommendations Put Forward in Dealing with IT Security Incidents," Gov.Sg, January 13, 2019, https://www.gov.sg/news/content/channel-newsasia---singhealth-coi-report.

14. Faris Mokhtar, "SingHealth Top Executive Hopes for New Solutions to Internet Separation, Which Has Caused 'Multiple Inconveniences,'" TODAY (Singapore), November 5, 2018, https://www.todayonline.com/singapore/singhealth-top-executive-hopes-new-solutions-internet-separation-which-has-caused-multiple.

15. Singapore Ministry of Communications and Information, "Public Report of the Committee of Inquiry," executive summary, p. v.

16. Ibid.

17. IHiS, "IHiS Committed to Improving Cyber Defence in Healthcare," January 14, 2019, https://www.ihis.com.sg/Latest_News/Media_Releases/Pages/Committed-to-Improving-Cyber-Defence-in-Healthcare.aspx.

18. Plutarch, *Plutarch's Lives, Vol III*, trans. John Dryden, "Life of Lucullus," paragraph 25; a slightly different account (the messenger was hanged) is in Appian's *Roman History XII, The Mithradatic Wars*, paragraph 84.

19. J. Richard, "Battle of Tigranocerta, 6 or 7 October 69 B.C.," accessed January 22, 2019, http://www.historyofwar.org/articles/battles_tigranocerta_69_bc.html.

20. Sean Martin, "Cyber Security: 60% of Techies Don't Tell Bosses About Breaches Unless It's 'Serious,'" *International Business Times*, April 16, 2014, https://www.ibtimes.co.uk/cyber-security-60-techies-dont-tell-bosses-about-breaches-unless-its-serious-1445072.

21. David Dayen, "How Twitter Secretly Benefits from Bots and Fake Accounts," *Intercept*, November 6, 2017, https://theintercept.com/2017/11/06/how-twitter-secretly-benefits-from-bots-and-fake-accounts/.

22. Linda Emanuel et al., "What Exactly Is Patient Safety?" *Advances in Patient Safety: New Directions and Alternative Approaches*, vol. 1 (Rockville, MD: Agency for Healthcare Research and Quality, 2008).

23. Ibid.

Chapter 10

1. Median dwell time = 101 days, includes the Americas, Europe, the Middle East, Africa, and the Asia Pacific. FireEye M-Trends 2018 Report, https://www.fireeye.com/content/dam/collateral/en/mtrends-2018.pdf; mean time to identify (MTTI) = 197 days, includes 15 countries/regions globally (n = 477 companies). Ponemon Institute, "2018 Cost of a Data Breach Study," https://databreachcalculator.mybluemix.net/assets/2018_Global_Cost_of_a_Data_Breach_Report.pdf.

2. US Cyber Command, accessed January 28, 2019, https://www.cybercom.mil/; Hacking Team, accessed January 28, 2019, http://www.hackingteam.it/.

3. John Pletz, "Keep a Close Eye on This Cyberterror Dispute between 2 Giant Companies," ChicagoBusiness.com, January 11, 2019, https://www.chicagobusiness.com/john-pletz-technology/keep-close-eye-cyberterror-dispute-between-2-giant-companies.

4. Liz Moyer, "Former Equifax Executive Charged with Insider Trading for Dumping Nearly $1 Million in Stock Ahead of Data Breach," CNBC.com, March 14, 2018, https://www.cnbc.com/2018/03/14/former-equifax-executive-charged-with-insider-trading-ahead-of-data-breach.html.

5. Hiroko Tabuchi, "$10 Million Settlement in Target Data Breach Gets Preliminary Approval," *New York Times*, March 19, 2015, https://www.nytimes.com/2015/03/20/business/target-settlement-on-data-breach.html.

6. Alina Selyukh, "Every Yahoo Account That Existed in Mid-2013 Was Likely Hacked," NPR.com, October 3, 2017, https://www.npr.org/sections/thetwo-way/2017/10/03/555016024/every-yahoo-account-that-existed-in-mid-2013-was-likely-hacked.

Index

Acknowledgments

We are indebted to our many clients, whose diversity in industry, geography, culture, and organization afforded us the opportunity to refine and test our work.

The support Harvard Business Review Press provided throughout the entire book production process has been wonderful. In particular, we want to thank Julie Devoll, who ensured continuity from the first book to this one; Tim Sullivan, who started the process; and Kevin Evers, who guided us through publication.

Finally, we thank our families. Our wives, Yang and Beverley, recognized the importance of writing this book and encouraged us on our journey. Our children, Martin, Jacqueline, Charlotte, and Natalie—and the future they represent—inspired us throughout. In turn, may this book inspire them to lead and effect change in the world they inherit.

About the Authors

Thomas J. Parenty is an international cybersecurity and privacy expert who, over the course of more than thirty-five years, has worked at the National Security Agency, testified multiple times before the US Congress, and advised government agencies and corporations across the globe. He is a cofounder of the cybersecurity firm Archefact Group and author of *Digital Defense: What You Should Know About Protecting Your Company's Assets* (Harvard Business School Press, 2003).

Jack J. Domet is a management expert with more than twenty-five years' experience in helping multinational corporations adapt to shifts in technology, globalization, and consumerism through organizational change. He is a cofounder of Archefact Group, where he focuses on building leadership and organizational capabilities in digital stewardship.